Vision to Reality

VISION *to* REALITY

Stop Working,

Start Living

CURTIS L. JENKINS

NEW YORK

LONDON • NASHVILLE • MELBOURNE • VANCOUVER

Vision to Reality

Stop Working, Start Living

Published in New York, New York, by Morgan James Publishing. Morgan James is a trademark of Morgan James, LLC. www.MorganJamesPublishing.com

Proudly distributed by Ingram Publisher Services.

Morgan James BOGO™

A **FREE** ebook edition is available for you or a friend with the purchase of this print book.

CLEARLY SIGN YOUR NAME ABOVE

Instructions to claim your free ebook edition:
1. Visit MorganJamesBOGO.com
2. Sign your name CLEARLY in the space above
3. Complete the form and submit a photo of this entire page
4. You or your friend can download the ebook to your preferred device

ISBN 9781631957574 paperback
ISBN 9781631957581 ebook
Library of Congress Control Number:
2021945729

Cover Design by:
Megan Dillon
megan@creativeninjadesigns.com

Interior Design by:
Christopher Kirk
www.GFSstudio.com

Morgan James is a proud partner of Habitat for Humanity Peninsula and Greater Williamsburg. Partners in building since 2006.

Get involved today! Visit MorganJamesPublishing.com/giving-back

I dedicate this book to my Uncle Bernard, who I loved so much.
His heart had no bounds, and I miss him so much.

TABLE OF CONTENTS

ACKNOWLEDGMENTS

My Uncle Bernard was more than just an uncle; he was like a brother to me. He was the youngest of all my uncles, and he had such charm. I always wanted the ability to melt hearts like he did when he met and engaged with someone. When he called me about his financial issues I knew something was wrong because he never came to me asking for money. When I was able to help him uncover the sources of these issues, I realized that I had been doing that for so long with companies that it had become a skill I could use to help more people. I was able to be there for him—like he was always there for me. That is why I dedicated this book to him. May he rest in peace!

To my significant other, Karen Tilghman, who had to listen to me talk about every facet of this book in conversations—late nights, early mornings, while driving, or at events—and still provided love and support to me while I completed this book. I am thankful.

To my mother, Arlene Wynder, and my Uncle Jr. (Leroy Jenkins Jr.), who asked me almost daily about my book—when it would be available to them and how they could help me with it. Thank you for always being there for me.

To Erik Truxon (Just It's Electric), Calvin R. Snowden, Jr. and Diedre A. Downes (BDFS Group), and Rich Vivirito and Shannon Watson (IT3)—who knew that when we got together to discuss business that you would help me shape my project management experience into something to help your companies grow that I can now leverage to help other companies grow? It was your companies that allowed me to serve as your advisory board chairs. Thank you for making me part of your businesses and allowing us to grow together.

To my League of Executive African American Professionals (LEAAP) brothers—Claude Demby, Claye Greene, Ty Hollins, and Kevin Fanroy—it is you who hold me accountable to my goals and challenge me to do more. You are why I stress that accountability is a gift and something everyone—especially an entrepreneur—needs.

To my friend and speaker's bureau leader, Nicole Anderson, who introduced me to the Ascendent group and Raoul Davis, who interviewed me and pulled the entrepreneur information out of me to create this book. Raoul also challenged me to be different, and that's when I created and trademarked the Realization Framework Experience˙. Thank you also to Maya Nazareth, my go-to person who helped me organize and create my podcast, Visionary Ventures!

To Kevin Lewis from The Everyday Entrepreneurs who allowed me to practice all elements of my Realization Framework Experience as a class with the members. You all helped me hone my messaging and what is relevant to entrepreneurs today.

To my editor, Aubrey Kosa, and your diligence to make sure I crossed all my t's and dotted all my i's. Your suggestions made this book easier to read. You are amazing and talented.

To the Morgan James Publishing family for believing in this book and helping me navigate all the ins and outs of bringing this book to the world, especially David Hancock, Jim Howard, Bethany Marshall, and my Author Relations Manager, Gayle West.

To the DENT group—Mike Reid and Daniel Priestley—your Key Person of Influence business accelerator course is the best I have ever taken in getting my business moving fast using your five-step methodology. I especially appreciate your support in helping me with the current title of this book. Your suggested change from the original title to the current title resonates so well that it also convinced my publisher, Morgan James, that the title will do better with all who encounter the book. Thank you for helping me make a DENT in the universe!

And to all those who dare to be great with growing your business. This book is for you. Remember, business is a team sport—you never travel alone.

A NOTE FROM THE AUTHOR

Vision to Reality is primarily intended for businesspeople—entrepreneurs who have already answered "why" they are in business and hope to learn the "how" to successfully grow their company. In the current era of digital marketing, there are thousands of thought leaders offering strategies for success and growth, but none of them have my unique expertise. Motivational self-improvement products and programs comprise a $10-billion industry that promises guidance in a plethora of areas from finance and business to health and wellness and spirituality, to name just a few. Amidst the self-help books, infomercials, seminars, workshops, webinars, and websites, The Realization Framework Experience° methodology stands apart, guiding readers to clear the fog and learn the skills they need to succeed in their business, no matter the industry.

Although my business background is primarily within project management, my expertise speaks to those in every industry. I have worked in both small businesses as a management consultant and in large companies as a consultant and as an employee. Across the board of sizes, companies have two main functions: operations and projects, and my experience has brought vision to reality in both of those functions. With the understanding that each entrepreneur has a unique vision, The Realization Framework Experience promises to bring that vision to reality with clear guidance and solid expertise.

It was through the execution of large, diverse projects that contributed to the growth of mid-size and large corporations that I learned my method of "vision to reality" could also apply to small businesses and entrepreneurs who did not have the means to hire large teams to execute their desired strategies. When I realized the same key components were crucial to success across the board, and that they could be achieved without a large cash position, The Realization Framework Experience was born.

In this book, I make the message clear and succinct so everyone—from first-time entrepreneur to seasoned businessperson—can learn and apply this novel approach. The guidance and wisdom are adaptable to each individual's unique vision, allowing their vision to become their reality. With the directions and solutions everyone needs to succeed in the business world, from solo entrepreneurs to billion-dollar companies, The Realization Framework Experience overcomes challenges and brings growth and success—when put into practice. It all begins with the first step: determining what your vision is and articulating that vision clearly for yourself and your team.

Note: The images used for examples may not always be easy to read; therefore, all images can be found on my website at: www.cljassoc.com.

For Entrepreneurs

Vision to Reality is designed to guide entrepreneurs to focus their efforts, ensuring every outcome contributes to the overall vision. For entrepreneurs facing an unexpected decline in growth or sales, or those experiencing other struggles in their businesses, The Realization Framework Experience will help return business to the growth phase, which ultimately leads to success. Entrepreneurs often find they face challenges because their area of expertise doesn't include all the necessary skills to grow their business successfully. In this book, the skills every entrepreneur needs to learn are presented with clarity, along with how to build and organize a team to get the job done and invest in building stronger customer relationships, internally and externally, with both customers and suppliers.

For Businesspeople at Every Level

This book explores using creativity and soft skills to pave the way to achievement for businesspeople hoping to rise to leadership positions and successfully attain their work and life goals. With more than twenty years of project management experience, I have come to understand that while there is no one-size-fits-all strategy for success, the five steps of The Realization Framework Experience can guide those climbing the corporate ladder over obstacles to achieve their unique vision of success. With customized strategies, leaders are shown how to make necessary behavior shifts, dispel fears, and leverage their skills.

For Seasoned Businesspeople

After working in project management for more than twenty years, I understand that projects are simply a subset of a business's overall vision, which means every project's underlying goal must be the achievement of the overall company vision. In business, there is nothing more important than ensuring every customer experience is exceptional. This book and The Realization Framework Experience explain how to invest in employees and customers for an edge over the competition. In today's world, the competition is more intense than ever before, extending its reach with the ability to serve customers from great distances. Competition is no longer limited by geographic location. Those working in businesses, from giant corporate entities to small local companies, can learn from the knowledge imparted in this book and successfully leverage The Realization Framework Experience to turn their vision into reality.

***

When you master the concepts in the book, you will be what I call a Visionnaire. You will have more money, more time, and more support. You will work less and live more! You will be known as someone who has achieved success in their business because they were able to create and live out the vision of their business. Visionnaires make themselves successful by making their vision a reality.

Please take the Visionnaire Scorecard at https://visionnaire.scoreapp. com/ to see where you are in your Visionnaire journey.

Are you ready to get started and move from vision to reality? Are you ready to be a Visionnaire?

Let's begin!

INTRODUCTION

James's career began fifteen years ago. He was recruited by a Fortune 500 company's marketing division right out of graduate school. All went well for James in business as he quickly climbed the ranks in the company, rising near the top. In his personal life, he had fallen in love, married, bought a house, and started a family. He seemed to be living the dream, but with each step forward came more responsibility and more stress. And yet, he wanted more; he wanted to achieve the real life of his dreams.

James wanted to start his own business. He had a great idea, a very marketable one. He felt becoming an entrepreneur was the answer he was seeking. He'd be his own boss, set his own hours, rise above the competition quickly, and have more time to spend with his growing family. He would be able to create the career and lifestyle of his dreams.

Five years into his new business, James the entrepreneur finds himself more stressed than ever, working constantly but never seeming to get ahead. He still believes the basis for his business is good, and he can't understand why growth hasn't followed inspiration. His finances are a mess, his employees come and go like the tide, and his company isn't making the powerful connections with customers he imagined.

Rather than setting his own hours, he feels as though his business rules him. Times of enjoying life with his family and friends seem a distant memory. He feels overwhelmed, on the verge of exhaustion, never able to take a break. He fears failure is on the horizon, but his wife and family are counting on him to succeed. James has no money living payroll to payroll, no time to enjoy life, and no support since he doesn't trust others and thinks he must do everything on his own.

He knows he must be missing something, but what is it? And how can he find it?

***

Can you identify with James? Are you an entrepreneur who is working hard but still not achieving your desired success? Do you find yourself wondering why?

The truth is that working hard, by itself, likely won't get you far. In most instances, you'll just end up like James—tired, overworked, stressed, and annoyed, still short of your vision for your business and your life.

No doubt, hard work should be part of the path to success, but hard work alone simply isn't enough. As it does for most things, growing older and wiser reveals new truths about hard work and success. Let's face it, there are plenty of excuses for failure. There is no shortage of justification for mediocrity. There are lots of disillusioned and frustrated entrepreneurs who have run headfirst into the challenges of successfully running the business of their dreams.

Just look at the rate at which entrepreneurs delve into self-help books, attend "How to be Successful" webinars and seminars, and also seek the assistance of mentors. And what do these less-than-successful entrepreneurs discover from their efforts to find answers? In most cases, they are presented with a myriad of reasons why their business has yet to reach its potential and succeed even though they have a great idea.

The reasons vary from seminar to seminar. Some entrepreneurs might be told their less-than-stellar efforts are rooted in an inability to adapt or change. Or they aren't flexible enough. They don't have the courage to take the necessary risks to succeed. They are fearful of stepping outside of their comfort zone, where their familiar circle of friends, colleagues, and acquaintances keeps them sheltered from new, better ideas. Others are told they can't simply rely on their credentials for success. Still others hear their lack of success is because they lack the self-confidence to push forward and achieve their vision. They are chastised for not understanding the fundamentals of finance, budgeting, or the value of time. They add more excuses to their list of reasons for their lack of success, while others continue to be masters of procrastination even though they appear to be working endlessly hard. Finally, there are those who are told they are falling short in business because they are trying to be 100 percent perfect.

Do any of those excuses sound familiar? Do you see yourself in these excuses? Are you struggling to succeed even though you spend most of your waking hours working—to the detriment of your life and family? Are you frustrated when no matter how much effort you put in, you still fall short of achieving your vision for a successful business and a better life? Do you want to make the necessary changes to move forward and live the life of your dreams?

Don't get the wrong idea; hard work is part of the path to success when coupled with authenticity and business savvy. But you need to realize there is more, and you'll never reach success by continuing to do what got you here.

It's been nearly eight years since I trademarked the term The Art and Science of Vision to Reality!® For me, that term is a way of life: taking entrepreneurs from one state into another, from vision to reality. My vision is improving the lives of humans in general, and my vision is achieved when others accomplish their own vision to reality. I want to see a world in which entrepreneurs give time to their visions to reality so that they have more money, more family time, and more support, a world in which they can stop working so hard and start living! Most of my business relationships or friends who owned their own business originally came to me wanting a loan because they thought their problem was that they needed more money. However, I found that they were either slow to pay me back or didn't pay me back at all, which was a problem. When I realized that I could help them better manage their businesses not by giving them money but by helping them understand their financial process shortcomings, that was the first step in helping them see their real problem and its symptoms. In some cases, I connected them with financial professionals to help them learn the language of business and money. In all cases, I employed my methodology and techniques to help them organize their overall business and stay cash-flow positive throughout their business journey,

The methodology process begins by encouraging entrepreneurs—like you—to visualize their futures. Where do you want to go? What do you aspire to? What do you really want out of life? Every entrepreneur's visualization is different, and every successful reality is unique. Once you can clarify your unique vision for the end goal—comfort, happiness, security, etc.— you can get started on the path toward the reality of success.

The bad news is that when you get to your successful reality, you develop the habit of going for more. Unless your goal is an outright exit strategy, you will see another future for your business. The dreaming never ends when you are a dreamer. However, despite never being satisfied with the achievement of successful reality, you will have one or more businesses operating the way you expect. Your employees, your finances, and your outcomes become more predictable. Life will be simpler, and you will continue growing in your next vision to reality adventure.

When your visualization becomes clear to you, your vision to reality journey can truly begin. The journey always begins with developing a plan of assessment. After assessment comes organization, which includes an entrepreneur's most valuable asset: people. The people can include team members, advisors, mentors, and customers. Each entrepreneur must learn to invest in individuals who are part of their vision, for each individual, in their own unique way, will determine the health and course of the business.

Once the overall vision is in place and the details are considered, entrepreneurs should spend some more time visualizing the future. It is there that The Realization Framework Experience (RFE) comes in, guiding entrepreneurs—like you—on the path to the realization of their vision. And it all starts with a simple statement: "Just Imagine …" Vision to Reality promises remedies for removing the roadblocks standing in the way of your vision, as well as avoiding backsliding when the going gets tough, and, finally, overcoming and realizing your successful future.

Entrepreneurs often experience challenges that keep them from success. Others take obvious steps forward only to find themselves backsliding into detrimental habits and cognitive dysfunctions like confirmation bias and status quo bias. Only a few achieve success and realize the vision that inspired them at the beginning. Vision to Reality will show you that although entrepreneurs face similar challenges, your pathway to success, like everyone's, is unique. The RFE is designed to help you find your one-of-a-kind path to success through five simple steps.

My inspiration for The Realization Framework Experience sprang from Desmond Tutu's famous wise words, "There is only one way to eat an elephant: a bite at a time." Tutu's quip refers to the fact that while often life seems challenging or disheartening, anything can be accomplished by taking one step at a time toward the goal. Entrepreneurs certainly know the wisdom of Tutu's words. Just visualizing an elephant on a plate makes the task of eating it seem insurmountable—and this is how entrepreneurs see their problems. The key is gaining the necessary confidence to take the first bite—or first step—to find a simpler path to success, one victory at a time.

Vision to Reality is designed to do just that: help you and other entrepreneurs begin taking the steps forward to ultimately accomplish their vision. Through the RFE methodology, I provide five easy steps on the path to entrepreneurial success, taking "one bite at a time."

Let's explore the methodology for a moment:

REALIZATION FRAMEWORK
E X P E R I E N C E®

The RFE consists of five steps to take you, in depth, from start to finish—from vision to reality. Through the methodology, you learn the best approaches to:

- **Visualize** the Future (Discover Your Aspirational Goals)
- **Evaluate** the People Directly Involved in Making Your Dream a Reality (You, Your Employees, Customers, Board of Advisors, etc.)
- **Calculate** and Assess the Needed Cash Flow (Budget, Balance Sheets, Income Statements, Cash Flow, etc.)
- **Clarify** by "Clearing the Fog" (Develop a Clear Plan for the Future)
- **Realize** the Future (The Happy Ending or Pathway to the Next Beginning)

Throughout this book, we will refer to this as the RFE or methodology. We will dive deeper into each component and bring them all together with examples in the latter portion of the book. *Vision to Reality* brings these concepts to life to help entrepreneurs overcome the obstacles and challenges they face in business, avoid backsliding into old negative habits, and ultimately achieve their dreams.

Succeeding in business is no easy task, but my approach, backed by many years of experience, can help each unique entrepreneur—including you—clear the fog and take the next logical steps forward toward the realization of their dreams. I love the imagery fog provides in this context because it is so understandable and easily visualized. In the fog, you can only see so far ahead, and you often cannot see the other side of the obstacle you face, much less your final destination. If you can clear the fog surrounding your future, you can actually see where you are going and take the steps to get there. In doing so, you also gain the ability to clear the fog for your team and help them to see what you see: your vision. Then, they can be as eager as you to get to a certain future.

Your successful reality is right in front of you on the other side of the fog. The RFE will take you on a journey, a transformation, a path from your vision to reality.

PART 1:

What Leads Smart Entrepreneurs and CEOs Astray?

Vision to Reality starts in a unique place—the place where most entrepreneurs stumble, the place where they are simply unable to get out of their own way. The truth is that all leaders—entrepreneurs, CEOs, and everyone in between—can be led astray to the point where they are working only in their business and not on their business. This book is a resource for readers to develop a growth mentality based on their vision, a new strategic plan, and a roadmap for how to get to the realization of their vision.

Each business must be brought to life by implementing new ideas and raised standards. *Vision to Reality* will help you become a better business owner, returning the joy, excitement, and passion you had at the beginning of your entrepreneurial journey. Let's begin your journey into the realization of your original vision as the charismatic leader of a successful business and a dream lifestyle with a look at some of the most common things that take leaders astray.

Chapter 1:
MISDIAGNOSED PROBLEMS

The world is overflowing with experts who are broke. Why is that? Often the reason for a business's failure, even the extraordinary business ideas that should work, is misdiagnosed problems or misalignments. In this chapter, we'll begin our exploration of the common issues faced by entrepreneurs, CEOs, and other business leaders by looking at misdiagnosed problems.

As most of us know, the coronavirus pandemic of 2020 resulted in many small businesses suffering. Some went out of business entirely, and others got the short end of the stick when it came to funds from the government. Knowing the world will be even more dependent on the success of small businesses in the future, I want you to be successful. To make sure that happens, you must develop into the charismatic leader you were meant to be with a future-based cause (e.g., sustainability), offering opportunities for your target customers. And I specifically say charismatic because you must be an inspiration to the people you want to follow you. You must inspire a compelling desire to participate in the journey with you. You must determine what is in it for others so that they support you and your goals.

Facing the Obstacles and Challenges of Leadership

As an entrepreneur, business owner, or CEO, you have likely already faced some of the obstacles and challenges that come with managing a business. You've also likely already encountered the difficulty of finding the necessary solutions. If you have been in business for any time at all, you have probably found yourself frustrated, dealing with similar issues time and time again, leaving you perplexed and wondering why the same issues keep coming up.

Why do the same challenges continue to manifest in your business? In many cases, the problem is misdiagnosis or misalignment, which can occur when you attempt to simply resolve the symptoms rather than find the core problem and its solution. It is quite similar to a medical problem when symptoms, like pain, are addressed, but the cause of the pain is not. If you fail to address the cause of the problem, you will find yourself continually facing the same issue again and again without resolution. Don't ignore the symptoms altogether, as they help you understand that a problem is looming, but you must face the problem head-on to resolve it.

The issues that are often misdiagnosed can also be the result of misalignments in the company. Generally, business problems that continually resurface are misdiagnosed issues coming from an undiscovered, underlying problem. The underlying issue could be poor cash flow, which is a result of not recognizing that your expenses are coming in faster than your income. Or it could be too much debt because you are constantly borrowing money from various sources just to make the payroll for the week or to keep the business running after an unexpected charge decimated your bank account. A misalignment could be marketing efforts aimed at an uninterested audience. The solution to these misdiagnosed issues is often found not by working harder or simply addressing the symptoms of the problem but in discovering the genuine source of the issue and resolving it with the appropriate course of action.

Identifying Misdiagnosed Problems and Misalignments

Entrepreneurs, CEOs, and other business leaders often blame problems on employees, customers, the industry, the market, the economy, etc. They don't think their employees are following the instructions from the top, but typically when they are asked what they are telling their employees and how they are guiding them, their answer includes one of these excuses:

- Well, I send an email and I have bullet points of instructions, guidelines, and goals.
- My employees fail to follow through and get the goals accomplished.
- When I get back to them, all they have is a bunch of questions but no answers.
- I do not have time to deal with them; I have important work/meetings that require my time.
- They need too much from me.

One of the main issues with misdiagnosed problems is entrepreneurs, CEOS, and other business leaders usually believe the issues are someone else's fault when, in truth, most business leaders are not spending enough time with their people to clarify their instructions and the business goals.

A similar issue arises regarding customers, specifically customers who aren't paying their bills. This issue, in turn, creates problems for the business's payroll and accounts receivable. When asked about the age or velocity of their money, they don't know the answer, nor do they have a plan for preventing the issue from happening again.

So, misdiagnosed problems often stem from leadership assuming the issue is one thing when, in reality, it is something entirely different. The answer for solving problems lies in taking the proper steps to diagnose the real problem the first time.

Diagnosing Problems Properly

Entrepreneurs and business leaders like you can solve problems effectively with a bit of listening and effort. The problem arises when you don't feel you have the time to reengineer a process, manage the process, and ensure a quality solution, but simple common sense and effective listening are often the first steps in avoiding misdiagnoses and misalignments in your business. Always listen to team members. Ask them about issues they are experiencing that make their jobs more difficult. When you have their answers, do not judge them or determine that those team members have weaknesses since they are living with the issue day-to-day. Listen to your team members and really think about the changes you need to make to improve misalignments and diagnose problems.

Many of the problems that arise in business are quickly blamed on others. On one hand, if your suppliers screw up, they are likely screwing up for both you and your competitors. While you can't fix a supplier problem directly, you can solve a few issues by simply asking for a solution to the supply problem with guarantees, altering your contract to include penalties when problems arise, or change to a higher-quality supplier. On the other hand, if your marketing department bombs, that's on you. You can only fix one of these problems effectively: your marketing department, the one over which you have direct control. Once you uncover the real cause of the problem, you can fix it. What you can't fix are the symptoms of the problem, at least not until you find the source.

Once you have diagnosed your problems properly as within or out of your control, how do you decide which issues are the most crucial to your business's success? There are two schools of thought on the answer. The first is that you solve the issue causing the most problems for your bottom line. The second is that you solve the problem most annoying to you. You choose, but in my opinion, as long as you are improving your bottom line, the annoying issues can wait!

Common Misdiagnoses and Misalignments in Business

In business, misdiagnoses and misalignments are more commonplace than most would like to admit. Here are some of the most common misdiagnoses and misalignments in businesses to look out for.

- A frequent area of misalignment is hiring, particularly among entrepreneurs and other small business owners. Many leaders running a small business make the mistake of hiring family or friends to help with the business, but the leaders don't follow through and spend time with their new hires to share the vision and mission of the company as well as set expectations. The misalignment quickly becomes evident as the new employees fail to meet expectations. For me personally, along with many other like-minded entrepreneurs, it took a long time to realize that other people aren't "like me"; they don't act upon or approach situations and circumstances in the same way I would. Ultimately, this means they are not as invested in my outcomes as I would like them to be. But you can hire someone who is not like you with a set of strengths that will get the job done. Focus on what you need, not how similar the person is to you. When hiring friends and family, for example, more often than not, their goal is primarily the financial compensation they receive, not necessarily the quality, quantity, or overall outcomes you desire. If you were in their position, you would put in the extra effort (because it's your business), and you expect that extra effort from them as well, getting upset when they fall short. They, on the other hand, feel they are going the extra mile for you, even if that doesn't match your expectations. The goal is not to lower your expectations but to ensure you match expected outcomes with the appropriate talent. Therefore, take a close look when you are hiring. Ask yourself if you would hire this family member or friend if they weren't connected to you. Don't skimp on the process of hiring the talent you need.

- Another common area of misalignment is compensation for talent. As business owners or entrepreneurs, we often believe that hiring as cheaply as possible helps the bottom line when, in fact, the reverse is true. Those who are **fairly compensated** for the quality of their work and their talent will do more—and do it better. But it is equally important not to overcompensate to help someone. If you go out of your way to help someone and they do not deliver to your expectations, you will be upset and disappointed. Your choices make the difference, so spend the necessary time to ensure you get the highest quality talent, and create an environment of open, honest communication to bring out the best in your employees. Often as small business owners without a large war chest, we test our employees, spoon-feeding them menial tasks for the matching menial compensation. Each task is a milestone or "carrot" to prove themselves. Because they have not yet proven themselves trustworthy, you don't want to share all the information required for the person to actually do their job and help your business. This is not a good tactic. Avoid it. It is a waste of time and money. An intern can follow this process because the cost is not that great, or you can do this once or twice with someone you know has great talent to see how they fit into the overall business. But when you make this process a norm, it is a recipe for disaster, at least from what I have seen.
- Promotion is another area of misalignment. While promotion should always be a consideration, do not build it into your plan and provide a false sense for employees that promotions are to be expected just because they show up. Create all the jobs you need and promote when an employee demonstrates they can do more,

take on more responsibility, and accomplish more than what you originally believed. Spend time finding the right person—the one who can perform all the duties in the job description. This is not someone who can only do some small jobs; they should have the potential to expand their skills and grow into other facets of the business. While it sounds good, promoting often will frustrate you because you will always have to be on the search for more talent, which can become a never-ending cycle.

- Failing to properly plan is also an area of misdiagnosis, as well as an area of misalignment. Failing to plan only allows you to focus on the present moment, the symptoms of your problems, and the current issues. Planning has the opposite effect. It helps provide a guide for your employees. It allows you to learn from the past, focus on the present, and look to the future, as well as giving you the opportunity to solve problems at the source, rather than suffering from misdiagnoses and misalignments and the setbacks that manifest as a result.

Chapter 2:

INABILITY TO GET OUT OF THEIR OWN WAY

As I mentioned in the list of common areas of misalignment in business, most entrepreneurs simply don't trust anyone to "do it like they do it." They can't get out of their own way. They often have a history of operating as solo entrepreneurs—always being the hero. This is the primary thief of your time as a business leader! As a result, the question they are often faced with is: "Do you want to run a business, or do you simply want another job?" In many cases, business owners may have created a business on paper, but, in reality, they haven't moved away from the position of employee and find themselves frustrated and wasting time getting in their own way.

There is no doubt that entrepreneurs, like you, are faced with numerous challenges, but more problems arise when you genuinely believe only you can solve the challenges and overcome the obstacles.

It goes something like this: an entrepreneur falls into the trap of not trusting anyone but themselves to do the work. They know their work got them where they are. They believe they can handle any situation.

Do you see yourself in this description?

In working with entrepreneurs, including myself, I ask them to list the top five areas that would make their lives easier if someone else could do them. But when work in those areas is assigned to an employee, the individual often fails to perform the task to the entrepreneur's expectations, and confirmation bias immediately kicks in! The employee failed to fulfill the task according to the entrepreneur's expectations, which results in the business owner shying away from future delegation. In other words, they can't get out of their own way.

Selecting the right talent is paramount for overcoming this issue. To help entrepreneurs see the issue clearly, I next ask if they believe the employee failed to perform the duties as expected because of a "skill" issue or a "will" issue. I often learn from interacting with both the entrepreneurs and their employees that failure to complete a delegated task is rooted in communication. The entrepreneur doesn't provide enough detail for the employee to meet their expectations, and because communication hasn't been fully established, the employee is afraid to ask clarifying questions. The entrepreneurs then latch on to the task when the employee fails to meet expectations, with the intent to never let go, thus their inability to get out of their own way.

A Lesson Learned from the One-Minute Manager

Years ago, I learned an important lesson from *The One Minute Manager Meets the Monkey*, a book by Ken Blanchard, William Oncken, Jr., and Hal Burrows. The book follows a familiar route: a leader challenges an employee to perform better or delegates tasks to an employee, which is followed by the employee failing to meet the challenge or task. This is often the source of a business owner deciding to just do everything themselves, knowing that approach will take less time than training employees and disciplining them to perform the task according to expectations. In taking this approach, owners are actually training their employees to dump tasks, problems, and issues (the monkeys) back onto the owners while still collecting their paycheck. In other words, the business owner is enabling employees to get their work done through the owner. This is smart on employees' part, but it can be very frustrating and time-consuming for the owner.

Changing the Nobody-Can-Do-This-Better-Than-Me Position

As humans, we gravitate toward the areas of work that provide the greatest satisfaction and the highest level of validation. Think about it. When you have a skill that you do well, having done it successfully for a long period of time, you become an expert in that skill. You enjoy what you do, particularly when you create a business or service based on your skill set. You also gain an inordinate amount of satisfaction. The result is large shots of dopamine are sent directly to your brain, making you feel good.

The problem arises when the feel-good moment is short-lived because you have to oversee and manage the overall business you hope to grow. Rather than enjoying the feel-good moment, you have to face the uncomfortable challenges required to move the business successfully forward.

It is then that delegation becomes one of the most important acts you can do as a leader—creating the necessary movement to achieve the vision you defined for the company. However, I have seen firsthand how leaders struggle with delegation. In one instance, I worked with a leader who refused to give up collecting payment for completed jobs. He also spent nights and weekends doing plumbing jobs, which could have easily been outsourced. In another situation, I worked with a leader who continually overpromised to his customers. He always provided reasonable, sometimes even aggressive, due dates to please his customers at the point of the initial discussion, but in the end, he always missed the due date he promised and offered not-so-good excuses. I worked with another leader who simply believed he was the only one who cared enough about the business to consistently get the job done right.

In the case of each of these leaders, I had to schedule extensive meetings to determine what their main issues were and address them. In each instance, two consistent issues became apparent. The first issue was that they never developed trust with their team members. Without a level of trust, their employees were never allowed to prove they could handle even the simplest tasks, much less the more difficult ones. The second issue was that they never developed a system with clear standards, operating procedures, and escalation paths for employees to follow, nor did they create job descriptions to ensure well-qualified individuals were hired who could actually perform the work.

Through working with these leaders, I was able to help each of them overcome these issues, referencing two key elements necessary to operate and manage a business successfully.

In the first example of the leader who did not want to give up collecting payment for completed jobs, it was a matter of actually showing him how by not insisting on collecting payment for jobs completed, his time was freed up to focus on more important aspects of his business. Rather than spending the time and effort to collect payments himself while struggling to make payroll, he could instead set reasonable payment schedules, ensuring jobs were completed and paid for on-time. The measurement used to set up the payment schedule was "days sales outstanding," and over a six-week period, he discovered that bringing this down to less than three days sales outstanding (DSO) resolved his collection issues. Next, we developed complete job descriptions for his employees and created a plan to hire a plumber on a full-time basis, keeping the owner from working nights and weekends. We achieved this by getting enough positive cash flow to hire the plumber after reviewing the cash flow on a weekly basis until there was enough momentum to take on this much-needed employee.

In this scenario, positive reinforcement was given to the leader every time they made their target of less than three DSO. Of course, when they didn't, I made sure the tone of the meetings suggested the leader was not behaving in the right way, even though I knew they were not happy about not getting the validation they sought. I had to spend a great deal of time understanding their overarching issues when it came to their financials and their employees. From that understanding, I created models of the success they could achieve if they followed the methods we determined were impacting their business.

In addition, I participated in the job interview process to help them find the right talent for the open positions. Next, I worked with them to develop their own unique set of Standard Operating Procedures (SOPs), which were crafted for onboarding the individuals they were hiring to take over specific duties.

This pattern holds true in nearly every scenario. In order to change the nobody-can-do-this-better-than-me position and rid yourself of the accompanying "monkeys," you must create a system with clear standards that your employees can follow. It is the only way to grow your business. With the system in place paired with talented employees, you can get out of your own way and trust your employees to take your ideas and run with them successfully.

One note is that I have seen this happen more with my service clients than clients who sell products. Service businesses are often developed by a person possessing a particular skill, such as a plumber, electrician, or general contractor. The overall goal for these owners is to grow their business and eventually put down their tools. In many cases, they also want to turn over their business to their children. To do so, they must work on the business, not in the business. However, they go to the jobs and do the jobs. In some cases, they do this twice because they follow up on work already performed by their employees. This is okay if that is what gives you satisfaction, but my clients tell me they want more. Another situation in which this happens often is when instead of training their office managers to collect cash or receivables, business owners do this themselves. These are both especially important areas to manage. In the first case, customers' expectations must be managed. Therefore, ensuring a job is done quickly and correctly, at or above customers' expectations is particularly important. However, this is often where the owner takes the wrong approach by involving themselves in work that does not add value to the business.

I have worked with many clients to develop standards for getting the job done correctly, including having their employees provide pictures at the end of the job. No pictures, no pay! Also, my clients have had foremen or project managers go to the customers and ensure the work is done correctly. Again, you must get the right talent and set the proper expectations. If you don't, you will pay for the job twice—through your employees' time and your own. I tell owners to value their time at $1,000 per hour and have them ask if the activity they are performing is worth that. If the owner continues to do everything themselves, employees get a free pass and become accustomed to being paid for mediocrity, and the owner spends too much of their valuable time. That's why the vision and processes are paramount to success so that everyone can perform their unique roles.

The same has happened with collections. I have taught numerous business partners to adopt what I dubbed the Roto Rooter method. When I had a leak, Roto Rooter came out and fixed it, but before they left my house, they required me to pay for the project on their mobile device. Many of my business partners provide invoices after the work is complete, and this is where I immediately see issues with collections. As a business owner, you need to get the money before you leave the site, along with direct customer feedback. If they weren't happy, the discussion should take place right there so the employee can learn. However, if you don't have a plan to collect and provide feedback, train one of your employees to collect money as a part of their job description. I have had business partners refuse to delegate this task to their detriment.

Finally, I almost always suggest hiring a sales team who can be trained to get more business—just like you do. In fact, they will probably do it better since this is what they do for a living. All of this requires the owner to get comfortable in being the leader—not a doer.

The system is built on *your* vision, and that vision must be translated clearly to your employees so they too can see it and join you in achieving the vision. For nearly every entrepreneur, including you, time is the enemy. For most entrepreneurs, maybe even you, conquering time is approached by resolving to spend more time doing the work themselves. The RFE is designed to help entrepreneurs use time to their advantage, resulting in better preparation, enhanced understanding, diagnosing problems effectively, better communication, and enhanced planning, giving entrepreneurs the tools they need to get out of their own way.

A Real-Life Example

I recently completed three months with a client helping him get out of crisis mode. He had just had one of his largest customers fail to pay for a completed project, and they were in court over the incident. The goal was to get the client out of crisis mode and back on track.

During the three months, we did a weekly cash flow exercise, focusing on the past week and the two weeks ahead with the goal to be a cash collection machine, building cash and cash reserves. *(I say "we" because when I partner with clients, I am all in on their behalf. Also note that I use client and business partner interchangeably throughout the book. We are in this together.)* We began working on cash collection as we looked forward to the new year. Around week six, it appeared as though we had thrown six weeks of work away, as there was only around $5 in his account.

To get to the heart of the problem, I asked the CEO, "Are you in the business of business development or cash collections?" I knew the answer but wanted him to say it aloud and understand it clearly.

He answered quickly, "Business development."

The issue was that once he put business development ahead of cash collection, he put his company in jeopardy because, at the time, he needed cash more than new business. But he gravitated toward business development. That was his sweet spot and where he got his validation, and running around to get cash from others became a norm that he was comfortable with.

During our weeks together, he hired an office manager with the goal to transfer all the responsibilities of cash collection to the office manager within two weeks. Two weeks passed, and he continued to put it off. He liked going to his customers after their projects were completed, running through a checklist, and collecting in person. He simply didn't want to give that responsibility away.

I posed another question to him, "Your vision was to be the largest minority contractor in the state, to be like Turner Construction. Do you really think the CEO of Turner Construction is running around doing cash collections?"

The question—and obvious answer—was a catalyst for him. I continued, "If you want to be focused on business development, you have to get out of your own way and let others take the responsibility for tasks like cash collection."

The moral of the story is that people often feel like they are doing what is necessary to save their business simply because they are "doing something" when nothing could be further from the truth. Most often they need to stop and take a step back. A Visionnaire always takes a step back during a crisis to get out of their own way.

Chapter 3:

WILLINGNESS TO MAKE EXCUSES

Entrepreneurs, business managers, and CEOs who make excuses for mediocrity in their businesses or for not hitting their goals have gone astray on the path to success. Excuses are often the results of a lack of plan, poor execution of the plan, and/or a lack of accountability and time management. Confirmation bias and status quo bias both lead to major excuses from business owners. The most blatant excuse I ever experienced with a client was, "It's everyone else's fault."

Poor execution is manifest when entrepreneurs and other business leaders fail to follow their own plan, don't follow through on discipline when it matters, and fall short of matching talent with the proper position (misalignment of personnel and work). When accountability is absent or falling short in the business, tasks are not accomplished, and exceptional ideas aren't acted upon in a timely manner. Accountability requires focus as well as discipline that is clearly defined and built into the business's systems and operations. Time management is also crucial to success in any business, and as mentioned earlier, time can be the enemy of entrepreneurial success. Everyone has the same amount of time each day, week, month, or year, so time cannot be among your excuses.

Clearly defining your plan and vision, training your employees well, and setting boundaries on your time can help you achieve success and bypass the excuses.

Avoiding the Mediocre Moments

Every entrepreneur faces mediocre moments or points in their careers when they are not meeting their goals. What they do in response to these shortcomings is what either leads them astray or guides them to success. Many respond to their shortcomings with, "I don't have enough time in the day. Yeah, I know I set this goal to be a million-dollar company, but everything I'm doing just isn't working. So, I'm just going to keep running as is." This response showcases another cognitive bias common among entrepreneurs: the status quo bias. The status quo bias says that it is better to keep things the same versus expending the energy and effort to look for better solutions. If not turned around, this bias can be the beginning of the end for a vision of success.

This point, where excuses rule, can be the give-up point, the point where entrepreneurs and business leaders become comfortable with the normal rat race. It is an acceptance of being uncomfortable that drives change. It takes practice, and here you will learn good practices. I teach every entrepreneur I work with that discomfort precedes success and that there needs to be a focus on continuous improvement to drive toward a better reality.

This point is also the point when business leaders lose their business and their independence and go back to simply having a job, becoming an employee in their own business. Instead of being the business leader who dreamed of running a successful business, they remain the sole person doing the very job they wanted to get away from when they started their new business. They get comfortable with their new job, forget about growing their business, and start making excuses. It is comfortable if this is what you want, but I am willing to bet it is not! Most of my business partners did not want what they had when I began working with them; they wanted more. The good news is that it doesn't have to be that way! But making excuses will not get you where you want to go.

Chapter 4:

▶ WORKING HARDER ▶

Most people think they can just put their head down and work harder to overcome setbacks and challenges. Entrepreneurs, CEOs, and business leaders are no exception. The truth is, when you approach setbacks and challenges this way, you commit more hours but only end up with more stress.

As an entrepreneur, business owner, or CEO, it is easy to see problems and simply resort to fighting fires instead of fire prevention. With this approach, every year you work harder and longer, but by itself, working harder, well ... doesn't work. Often the obstacles and setbacks you are hoping to overcome through hard work are really trying to force you to look for and develop a new strategy.

A Real-Life Lesson from Uncle Bernard

One day my Uncle Bernard, like many of my initial clients, called me up and asked to borrow some money. I agreed, saying, "Sure, you've never asked me for anything, but can you tell me why you need the money?" I always ask this question and require a good answer. Uncle Bernard had already told me the symptom of his problem: he could not pay his mortgage.

He hesitated, but then answered, "Well, I want to keep my house." I replied, "Okay, no problem." I gave him the money.

His house was saved—or so I thought.

Six months later, he called and asked again—symptom reemerged.

I replied, "Wait, you obviously have a problem. We need to get to the root of your problem. Uncle Bernard, one thing I do very well is dissect problems, so I'm coming to your house."

I immediately rented a car and drove five hours to visit him, leaving around 4 a.m. We causally talked and went to have breakfast at this great restaurant he wanted me to experience. I guess this was to ease into the discussion. I sat down with him and my aunt to discover the root of their problem, not simply continue to treat the symptoms.

After doing a forensic analysis of their income and expenses (cash flow) to see the full story, I discovered their finances were telling me the cause: they were running a $972 deficit each month. They were paying out faster than money was coming into their accounts. They had loans they could not possibly pay off with the minimum payments they were making. They were even trading off months when it came to who to pay that month, skipping a month for one creditor to pay another creditor, then back to the first creditor the next month.

Prior to my discovery, my uncle had envisioned a path to the supposed solution. He thought he only needed to work more hours for overtime, but this also created a great deal of stress. Without understanding the real problem, he began a terrible plan and did not clear the fog on his growing deficit due to the structure of his loans with very high interest rates. He was also using payday loans, a position you can never work your way out of. His ultimate plan was to work and work and continue the churn.

Instead, I advised him to focus on more revenue with what he had but not with more hours of work. I suggested, "Here's your opportunity to rectify the situation. First, you have a big house, so why not rent out rooms?" They had talked about this previously as an option, but they never drummed up the courage to actually do it. I did this with my home. Renting out rooms is an excellent opportunity if you can handle others coming into your home. Next, I focused on the cost side of his issue, saying, "Let's figure out how to get rid of some of your extra costs." I saw that they had two cars and advised them to get rid of one. I received a lot of resistance to this course of action, but they were paying for a car they weren't really using. This was another emotional hurdle they had to get over.

After reviewing all their income and expenses, I showed them how the "work harder" plan would have had him working himself to death without paying off the debt. The plan I put in place would have them in the positive after a few years, improving their cash flow with no additional work hours needed. Finally, we made a plan for any large sums of money coming in, such as an IRS refund, and how it could be used to help decrease the deficit. The plan included who to pay first, how much to pay, and what to do next.

The same principle applies in business. You must get to the root of the problem, then plan a sensible, smart strategy, including what-if scenarios, to create greater opportunities without assuming the only solution is to work harder. Sadly, Uncle Bernard passed away from underlying health issues that he did not share until it was too late. He was used to keeping things to himself. The problem could have been diagnosed earlier, and he would have had a chance for survival.

Hard Work is a Good Start

Now don't get the wrong idea here. Hard work is a good start to growing a successful business. But hard work without a solid plan isn't likely to get you where you want to be. You need to be teachable, you need to be dedicated, and you need to work smart.

Arnold H. Glasow, well-known American entrepreneur, summed it up nicely: "Success is simple. Do what's right, the right way, at the right time." Hard work, aspirational vision, authenticity, inspirational leadership, and planning make up the foundation on which achievable successes are attained. The methodology is ready to take you from your vision to the reality of your success. Experiential knowledge from consistent try-and-try-again efforts is an important part of the path to success. Every experience is another step, another opportunity for you to learn and grow. It is the foundation on which the RFE was developed.

My experiences and understanding began as trial and error helping others grow their businesses. I started with helping my friends—entrepreneurs themselves—who came to me seeking to attain similar results as I had, which was success. What they failed to see behind my success was the planning, organization, communication, and hard work that got me there. In fact, as I worked with these entrepreneurs, I realized they had yet to cast their vision forward, lacking focus on where they wanted to go specifically and successfully. I had to explain that there is no straight line for anyone, and the path is different for everyone.

Every company grows in unique ways. Every business operates successfully with a variety of techniques. All entrepreneurs and their companies, including yours, go through trial and error and lots of hard work to discover what brings success for them. One lesson that must be learned early regardless is to focus on the people—the employees, the customers, and the advisors if you have them. Advisors are those who have been in your shoes, and they can be very helpful in removing roadblocks to your success, whether you see the roadblocks or not. Advisors are crucial for a successful scenario and keep you from having to work harder when you can learn from their mistakes.

The second lesson that is important to learn early is that fear can hinder growth and success. Whatever the source of fear, entrepreneurs must not run from fear but rather embrace it. My goal is to bring these truths to life, especially the truth that fear—gut-wrenching, in the pit of the stomach fear—is a surer sign of growth than hard work. Remember what I said earlier about discomfort preceding success.

The RFE is designed to make the difference in how you grow your business. While hard work is certainly part of the experience, it isn't all there is!

Business Growth and The Realization Framework Experience

Everyone's talking about Business Growth, right? We all know the coronavirus pandemic halted income for many businesses and even forced some into bankruptcy. Business growth is the whole point of the RFE. The RFE is not about working more hours to develop more business to help you create a seven- or nine-figure business model; it's about setting up your business to expand and contract easily based on ever-changing market conditions. But that can only happen if you stop trying to do everything yourself and leverage the talent in your organization and relationships to help grow the business. When used every day, the RFE can help you execute your business strategy successfully, adjusting as needed, without working yourself to death.

Chapter 5:

RANDOM GOALS

Simon Sinek wrote a book called *Start with Why*, saying, "People don't buy what you do; they buy why you do it." With that said, I never understood why people would make random goals without fully understanding their why. I know entrepreneurs do this because I often have to ask why they stated their goals in the manner in which they did—a manner that appears to be random and mostly unachievable. People make goals all the time. Sadly, most of the time they pick random numbers to attach to those goals simply because they sound good to everyone around them. These goals are often nebulous and unclear. Often, the response to my further questioning is something like "I just want to be comfortable" or "I just want financial freedom." Instead, business leaders need to set solid objectives with a daily, weekly, monthly, and quarterly basis to track their progress.

Your goals are so important for understanding the breakdown of your vision; they cannot be random. As an entrepreneur, you cannot simply state a random goal. How can you tell whether your goal is random? Random goals can be identified easily when the person stating the goal does not have the ability to articulate the goal's objectives or a reasonable end. One of the reasons I like to look at SMART goals specifically (Specific, Measurable, Attainable, Relevant, and Timebound) is because this framework easily explains how to set goals successfully. It is not a new concept.

Many times, business leaders are, rather than stating goals, making statements they feel will take away some level of pain. The pain is most often due to the difficulties and challenges they are experiencing in business, thus the common goal of making several million dollars. By stating this random goal, entrepreneurs believe they will experience a change in lifestyle and business with no more struggles to meet payroll, pay bills, or grow the business. They see the several million dollars as the solution, one in which more money means a booming business and flourishing lifestyle. In other words, the random goal is designed to take away the pain.

When working with business partners to clear the fog, we focus on the "why" of the goals. To do so, we home in on why they want to achieve the goal and why the goal makes sense for their business. I spend time with them, encouraging them to articulate the goal in a way that both makes sense to them and can be easily understood by someone else (me, in this instance). I don't validate goals but rather challenge the goal to clear the fog and help them develop a plan around the goal with a set of objectives using the RFE.

When stating actual goals, there is a process of risk assessment and mitigation. It is a crucial process to ensure we clearly understand all the factors keeping us from meeting those goals and what actions are required to clear the way. We then work together on a set of actions to help us meet those goals, identifying what needs to be done on a daily, weekly, monthly, and quarterly basis.

Knowing your "why" is much more important than setting a random goal. The idea is to get to the real driver behind the random goal—which is, in most cases, dealing with current pain and finding a way out of it.

An Example of Setting Goals

For an example of setting actual goals, I once had a client whose goal was to make $1.2 million in a single year.

My response to him was, "Why that number? What does that look like?"

He had no idea. It was a goal without any objectives or a sound strategy. It was a very ambitious goal, much like "I want to double my company's growth each year for the next three years" would be.

This is the key reason I focus on Vision. With a vision, you discuss your "why" as you articulate the vision. The random goal for this individual was to get to $1.2 million in revenue from a revenue closer to $300,000.

When I asked him why that number, he responded, "I want a million-dollar business." But what he really wanted was status and a feeling of success. He had not accomplished his goal in the last ten years of running his business.

Now what he wanted might have been achievable, but I needed to understand more. When talking about goals, you must start with what you envision—from types of customers to types/roles of employees, revenue, and companies and industries you hope to emulate.

For example, the Vision may be to run one of the largest firms in the United States, like (insert firm here). This company may have annual revenue between one and three million or even more. So my client might want to grow the company to $1.2 million and service more residential customers while also expanding into commercial contracts and government contracts like (insert firm here) does.

After breaking it down, I was able show my business partner that he first needed to stabilize his business. In stabilizing his business, he would bring in $30,000 a month based on his current operation, though it was currently way up or way down each month. In one year, after stabilization, that amounted to $360,000. This was a stretch goal to smooth out his business and average $30,000 per month, especially during the summer when his revenue profile would shrink based on his current contracts. However, this stability would provide enough comfort for him to focus on the next level of goals.

I went on to explain, "If we can get a small bump in incremental growth to $50,000 per month, then we can get to half of your number." I showed him how to break it down on a daily, weekly, monthly, and quarterly basis and analyze it regularly. I taught him how to make the necessary adjustments to reach his goal. Essentially, with my methodology, and in a short time, I showed him what his $1.2 million looked like day-to-day and how to get there.

Sample goals to grow the company to $1.2 million:

1. Develop new business service segments by the end of (Month, Quarter, or Year):
   a. Commercial: $500K (Customers)
   b. Government: $500K (Customers)
2. Hire three new sales team members (employees) by end of (Month, Quarter, or Year):
   a. Sales Manager
   b. Commercial Sales
   c. Government Sales
3. Stabilize the business by the end of year one to ensure a steady book of monthly business of $30,000
4. Grow the business by the end of year two to ensure a steady book of monthly business of $50,000
5. Transform the business by the end of year three to ensure a steady book of monthly business of $100,000 (strong business in commercial and government arenas picks up in year two)

His is simply one example of clearing the fog around random goals, drilling down into the specifics to make a goal an achievable stepping stone on the way to making your vision a reality.

Chapter 6:

OVERESTIMATING BANDWIDTH

E ntrepreneurs and CEOs are often guilty of overestimating their time, their bandwidth, and their ability to execute. The word bandwidth is a technical term, which in the digital age essentially means the volume of information a medium can handle. For example, a larger bandwidth can handle more data in a quicker, more efficient manner than a smaller bandwidth. In business, bandwidth is your capacity to accomplish work.

When I led a project management office, I was often asked to help develop a resource plan to support the business strategy. One of the ways I used to select talent was their ability to handle large projects or many projects—up to $10 million per project manager. When the business leaders asked me how much we could get done, I would tell them that we were positioned to manage $100 million in projects concurrently. However, that was just considering the project managers. Bottlenecks often occurred with other resources working their day jobs whose time was in demand. If I hadn't made the leaders aware of those constraints, they would have expected me to deliver on all those projects simultaneously. I had to work with them to develop a prioritization list so that I took care of the more impactful projects first. I refused to overpromise and underdeliver.

Many business leaders in small companies do not have an accountability mechanism in place and try to do it all, i.e., overestimating their bandwidth. In doing so, they fail to account for the full time, resources, and ability needed to execute their strategy or plan. This situation often happens as a company expands. For instance, an entrepreneur who did their job well when they were the sole entity might fail to execute when they begin to expand, often because they underestimate how much time they need to accomplish their goals, as well as overestimate the capabilities of those they entrusted with various roles. Time is lost switching from being a hands-on worker to performing leadership duties. Entrepreneurs must make this switch as early as possible and fight to stay in the leadership role. One tool that is helpful for staying in the leadership role is the Eisenhower matrix, which helps entrepreneurs with prioritization of urgent, important tasks that take up their time. It can be used to focus priorities on the necessary growth activities and delegate the lesser, but necessary, activities.

A Classic Example

A truly classic example of overestimating bandwidth is individuals hoping to work their way out of a difficult situation. Take an entrepreneur who does everything—business development, going on the job, picking up their tools, inspecting their employees' tools, accounting, payroll, and customer service—only a few of which tasks actually need to be accomplished by them. My teachings are about how to leverage others to help you. Tim Ferriss's book *The 4-Hour Workweek* is perfect here, and this is derived from his work. Look at what needs to be done and what your strengths are. Then delegate, delegate, delegate!

In one example, my client's strength was in business development; he is an expert in getting business. The problem arises in letting go of the menial tasks that take him away from acquiring new business. The other issue is transitioning him from wanting to work in a "nice little job," which is great, and you can have that if that's what you want. But he can't run a business and have a job in a way that will make him successful.

People stretch themselves too thin. Imagine you have real-life situations come up—and they do come up all the time. My client's wife had a baby, and it was a challenging few weeks for his business. He had not turned over the reins enough to keep his business running in his absence. That created stress between him wanting to be there for his wife and baby and wanting to keep his business running. I watched his business income slowly decrease while his stress was rising.

When considering the vision to reality, this is an area you must address first. Stop overestimating, thinking that you have all the time in the world. In fact, you don't have time for most of what you think you have time for.

Think of one thing you can do that will make a big difference in what you are trying to achieve. In this scenario, the one thing my client could have spent his time on was training someone else to do cash collection and customer service. That's it. This is why it is so important to focus on part three of the RFE: your people. You have to get the right people. The right people make all the difference, and that is where the investment needs to come in. Sometimes it comes through trial and error, but you must see yourself as the puppet master to get the right people doing the right tasks in your business. Doing so provides you the opportunity to grow. You can give the right person more capacity to get more done. Your goal should not be to have a full day by yourself—a to-do list with five tasks you must accomplish that you will never get done.

Humans, in my opinion and experience, are very poor estimators, especially of their time. Just five minutes extra with a customer spent chitchatting can be good for that customer relationship but bad for the next customer you are serving. Stop overestimating your time and commit to one, maybe two, tasks to accomplish in a day. The rest of your time is spent checking whether your employees did *their* one or two primary tasks that matter most to the business. Emergencies do come up, but if you develop a habit of doing the most impactful tasks on a regular basis, you will already be equipped to handle emergencies.

Get rid of the things that don't add value. When I am working with business partners, we discuss what adds value. Collecting money always adds value. Getting more business always adds value. Training your employees to do more always adds value. Look at how your time can garner the most value. Riding around in your car all day does not add as much value as leveraging technology and getting tasks done more quickly. I know some people like the personal touch, but be aware of the times we live in and do your best to leverage the available tools and techniques to help you get more done. Face-to-face can be good—but it takes time. Use your time wisely and don't overestimate how much of it you have in any given day.

Chapter 7:

UNDERESTIMATING CAPABILITY

Business leaders often go astray when they underestimate their capabilities. And entrepreneurs often underestimate their own capabilities: what they're capable of with the right leverage. What do I mean by leverage? In business, leveraging strategies include financial stability as well as enhanced business success.

Underestimating Versus Overestimating Capabilities

Business leaders make one of two mistakes: overestimating or underestimating their capabilities. As mentioned in the previous chapter, entrepreneurs tend to overestimate their capabilities when they have been doing all the jobs employees would normally handle in a company by themselves. It is hard for them to let go—to delegate responsibilities—out of fear of losing control. Other entrepreneurs underestimate their capabilities because they fail to leverage them. There are so many areas a business owner can leverage, many more than they believe possible.

For instance, leveraging debt is often underestimated. There is good debt and bad debt. An example of good debt is when an entrepreneur can leverage debt to purchase an asset, and the asset then brings more value to his organization and helps him grow his business. Assets generate income. This is just one positive form of leveraging; there are others. For example, a minority-owned or woman-owned business has leveraging power that often goes unused. Larger corporations look for diversity and can gain more business by working with a small business owner with a Minority, Women, and Disadvantaged Business Enterprise (MWBE) designation. In this situation, the small business owner with this designation has the power, which shouldn't be underestimated.

Business owners can also leverage relationships. In some cases, people who are working in their businesses are afraid to ask for help—and rightly so. Some business owners use money requested from family members or friends to put a Band-Aid on the business. But in opposition to those types of scenarios, business owners can leverage relationships by seeking assistance from other businesses instead. Business leaders spend lots of time networking and developing strong relationships, and when they do, they often find other companies to merge on projects and deals in ways that benefit both companies. One leader masters his capability, the partner leader masters her capabilities, and the synergy between the two allows for greater growth.

An Example of Leveraging Relationships

For example, one of my business partners was continuously trying to figure out how they were going to grow without the capital they needed. The company was getting business on the books but struggling to raise capital. All the other capital reserves had been tapped out. In several discussions with another company that needed to garner more business in the space of minority participation, my business partner and this other company came together to formulate a mutually beneficial solution through the formation of a separate third company.

In doing so, they worked a deal in which the larger jobs could be supported with the funding they needed. The primary company was able to execute as required and began to build their business to the point they no longer needed capital infusions. Together, they were equipped to take on more work. The last time I talked with them they were looking at a deal with a combined worth of $20 million—quite a step up for a business previously earning $2.5 million! They are a prime example of how you can take your capabilities—never underestimating them—and create the partnerships that allow you to grow your business.

Leveraging Capabilities Wisely

Consider this. I, like any entrepreneur, can grow my business—or, at least, my assets—through leverage. If I buy one house valued at $150,000 with a 30 percent down payment, I now have an asset worth $150,000 or more. Now, of course, I also have the liability associated with it, but because I am using leverage, I can put myself in an even better position to refinance the house and gain even more. So, I can grow my assets with leverage.

I once worked with a real estate entrepreneur who needed $80,000 to buy a multi-unit apartment building. He was tapped out with banks and other lending opportunities. After reviewing his personal and business finances, I advised him to consolidate his investments into one account, and he borrowed the money on margin against his stock portfolio. In less than ten years, he sold the apartment building for over $700,000. Today, I might have advised him differently because I know more, but it paid off. This was just one way for this entrepreneur to leverage his capabilities, but there are certainly other ways to leverage what you already have to raise capital for your business—without owing someone else!

Leverage allows individuals to use debt to their advantage. People don't know how to use debt to grow their businesses; they often only know how to use debt to pay other debt—a problem that results in an endless cycle of debt that doesn't add anything to the business.

One of my goals is to help people understand how to leverage debt to grow. For example, I recommended that a group of struggling entrepreneurs borrow $130,000 for one year with the purpose of funding a sales force for their companies. For that amount of money, they could, in most instances, get a sales manager and three salespeople to focus on gaining customers and enhancing sales. Their break-even point was then $130,000, and they are well on their way to meeting their goal of $1 million or more in sales because they leveraged their funding and hired the necessary sales resources to reach their goals.

Chapter 8:

LACK OF CONTEXT

I n business, lack of context means an inability to communicate effectively. In any company, context gives businesses the ability to communicate effectively with customers. Lack of context means the opposite. For example, without the appropriate context, your message will likely fail miserably or lead to miscommunication. Think about politicians whose words are taken out of context. Anyone can twist their words to mean something completely different than intended if those words are taken out of context. Every message requires good content and content delivery. In either instance, lack of context often results in mixed messages, which is never good for business.

So, if context is everything, does that mean lack of context is nothing? No. What lack of context actually means for entrepreneurs is lack of communication. And whether you are trying to communicate with employees or customers, communication is key to growing your business. Communication is how entrepreneurs tell their story, which, in turn, should inspire employees to work smart and encourage customers to action.

A Step-by-Step Guide to Improving Communication

When you start on the path to improve communication in your business, you must begin with listening skills as the first area to develop. Listening is one of the most crucial habits to be learned by and instilled in a leader.

For example, I did a training with one of my business partners who called to discuss firing an employee because the employee was ineffective. He wanted validation from me for firing the employee. I asked if I could interview the employee to get his perspective on why he was unable to complete his tasks. My client agreed. During the interview, I discovered the issue was not that he was a bad employee, nor was he not dependable. The employee needed more communication from my client—on a consistent basis. The employee also needed to learn more skills. In particular, he wasn't good with Microsoft Excel, so he was unable to create good reports with the calculations my client needed. The employee also had not been made aware of any of the organization's overall goals. Without that knowledge, he was unable to tie his overall duties into the larger picture of advancing the company. To resolve this issue, I developed a plan with my client. Part of that plan included creating an overall set of values and a weekly meeting agenda to set the tone for the week that included:

1. What needed to be done/completed, i.e., old work
2. What needed to begin/be completed this week
3. Resolution plans for customer issues
4. The employee's concerns, needs, and opportunities

Following the creation of this meeting plan, I met with the client's team. For the first month, I read the company's values and ran the meetings. After that month, I handed the meeting over to my client, offering support as needed. After the second month, I dropped to only attending meetings quarterly to get an update on progress. The goal of having my client meet with the entire team is to keep him from backsliding.

Here are the minutes from Client #1's meeting:

In Attendance: Client #1, Employee C, Employee D, Employee R, Employee M
Not in Attendance: Employee D2, Employee M2, and Employee T

Client #1 opened the meeting with a roll call and had everyone do a thirty-second introduction. He then established his commitment to the team and acknowledged the fine job they had been doing. He encouraged them, explaining that work would soon pick up. He introduced Curtis Jenkins, Jenkins & Associates, Inc.

*I then took the floor and acknowledged that everyone's time is valuable and promised to add value for the use of their time. I provided some background information as follows: Management Consultant with over twenty years' experience, created a trademark called "Vision to Reality." I explained that my skill set included taking my own or someone else's **vision** and making it **real** by:*

1. ***Attacking Change** head-on*
2. *Analyzing people need,*
3. *Instituting financial measures*
4. *Overcoming roadblocks and pitfalls*

*I explained I would do my best to make it a positive experience while we grew the company together. I explained that **I refuse to settle** for anything less than being the best and that they should also **refuse to settle.***

I explained to the team that the weekly meetings were to improve communication and collaboration, develop a team culture, and set expectations for the week, as well as provide time to have their voices heard.

I went on to explain that my client, their employer, needed their commitment and values, including full cooperation and adherence to the company's values, which included:

1. **Consistency** *– Delivering quality service, consistently delighting customers, and growing their own skill sets personally.*
2. **Reliability** *– Being on time, on budget, and providing everyone with a sense they are team players who can always be counted on.*
3. **Positivity** *– Approaching their work with a great attitude that is also reflected to the customers and team members.*
4. **Attention to detail** *– Ensuring nothing is left to question by customers and showing they care by taking care of the little things that mean a lot. No mistakes.*
5. **Honesty** *– The cornerstone of all relationships is trust. Being upfront and transparent about everything is key to be successful together.*

In addition, employees were encouraged to make suggestions for the company improvements, making it a company they would want their children to work for when they were growing up.

After my comments, the client made the following company announcements:

- *The office manager, employee K's, last day was Thursday*
- *The staff needed to provide scheduled availability*
- *Employee M introduced the TSheets, the new employee sign-in process, and explained when training was planned*
- *What needed to be accomplished in the coming week:*
  - *Monday: Be prepared with input at these meetings. Meetings start at 7:00 a.m. Goal is to end them as quickly as possible so they can focus on the important items. The company is paying for two hours when attending this meeting, no matter the length of the meeting.*

- *Tuesday: Small one-day job TBA morning—two men, one must be experienced.* **(Agreed upon by Employee A and Employee D)**
- *Wednesday:*
- *Thursday: Office cleanup/organization* **(Agreed upon by Employee A and Employee R)**
- *Friday:*

- *Three primary employees are needed to grow the company: actions the client is taking to grow the company and people needed.*
  - *Office Manager – goal by 11/1 or sooner*
  - *Reliable Estimator – goal by 1/31 or sooner*
  - *Project Manager – goal before end of Q1 2021 – based on business growth*

A roundtable discussion followed, including these comments:

- *Employee D: The future is yours as an electrician given all the new technologies like Electric Cars, Television w/o Cable, etc. He is willing to help you grow in this business. All you need to bring is the desire.*
- *Employee A: Wants to grow into an Apprentice and Electrician. He will research what it takes to get to those milestones and work a plan with the Client and myself to get on this career path.*
- *Overall, the remaining team members expressed their positive sentiment regarding the meeting and willingness to accept the challenge to grow the company.*

The meeting adjourned with the admonition to remember the company values and refuse to settle. This example went on for the rest of the year, and my client's communication with the company improved immensely. Employees got to have a voice and participate in the growth of the company because they felt the vision of the company connected to what was important to them personally. Do not underestimate the power of communication. You can easily create a communication mechanism for your teams. Start by bringing just these two items to the table: your vision and your values. Give the team an opportunity to provide their input and ideas. Make the meeting quick and purposeful and end the meeting positively! Afterward, your team will feel good and be ready to do great work.

Chapter 9:

COGNITIVE DISSONANCE

Cognitive dissonance is often defined as the performance of an action that contradicts your personal values or ideas, like when entrepreneurs want to hire the very best talent but pay them little to nothing for their skills.

Entrepreneurs' cognitive dissonance rears its ugly head quite often in their hiring practices. Entrepreneurs want to hire geniuses but underpay them for their expertise. They want the best talent, but they undercut their companies because they don't research what other companies in the industry are willing to pay. So they look at hiring the best talent in the form of someone's friend or relative, and they pay them peanuts. They can't gain success because of their cognitive dissonance.

One of my business partners had always used the "friend" route for hiring. Over the years, this was disastrous, resulting in a lot of failed relationships. Finally, I convinced him a temporary agency would save him lots of time, as well as heartache, if the hire didn't work out. A temporary agency also offers value and allows entrepreneurs to build strong relationships. Later he told me the temp was the best hire he ever had, and although he had to swallow the extra cost of the salary and agency fee, the returned productivity was well beyond what he expected. This was a great business relationship for the company.

When entrepreneurs develop relationships from the start rather than starting with an existing personal relationship, they get employees who are skilled, plus they save time and money because they don't have to upskill the friend of a friend or attempt to get away with lowballing top talent. In the end, hiring poorly takes entrepreneurs away from running their business.

I've found that this same cognitive dissonance rings true when people call my company. They want me to sit down with them, spend my time, and deliver a miracle for their company, but they don't want to pay. The truth I learned quickly is that when they have to pay me, they are more likely to listen to my advice and achieve their goals.

Exploring Cognitive Dissonance

Another way cognitive dissonance manifests in the workplace is in the concept of change management. Change management says a leader can bring the solution to people, but sometimes a leader has to bring the people to the solution. For example, let's say you added a new accounting system and were training everyone to use it, but everyone wanted to keep doing it the old way because they were comfortable. Change is, after all, uncomfortable, even when you know the change is for the better.

When it comes to cognitive dissonance, status quo bias and/or confirmation bias often comes into play. For example, let's say the new accounting system you implemented has an issue because someone entered incorrect data and totally threw the system off. One of your employees immediately says, "Hey, I knew this wasn't going to work." Their mind should be responding with, "Let me find out what the issue is, what the root cause is." But, in my experience, employees typically respond with, "Yeah, that's why I didn't want to go to that system because look at how it screwed up my numbers," rather than fixing the few input errors and seeing how much time and effort is saved.

Change is always required to move forward. The pushback you get is because people don't want to change.

With one client, we began with a discussion about cash collection. I often focus on cash collection because as entrepreneurs, my business partners are essentially running a finance company, not a business surrounding the product or service being provided. Entrepreneurs must have cash in and cash out, so I use these two measures: DSO (days sales outstanding), which is measured against DPO (days payable outstanding). Both measures help entrepreneurs understand their working capital and the speed at which money is coming in and going out. The idea is that the business should be collecting money faster than it is going out. In other words, DSO is shorter than DPO. Entrepreneurs don't often see money going out because they set a lot of their systems up for recurring payments, feeling like the automation helps them focus on the costs for the job/product and payroll. But by not measuring DSO, they aren't collecting the cash, or maybe they are giving customers due dates that are then missed by the customers.

One of the actions I take with my business partners is setting up the measures and showing my clients the projects on which they should have already collected rather than being in a mad scramble to get the money and make payroll. Often the projects were owed payment more than two weeks earlier. These measures come in handy when it's time to have a look at why money is leaving faster than it is coming in. One of the best solutions in this situation is putting in a POS (point of sale) system that requires payment right away. I recommend this to business partners, as well as a plan for the office manager or administrative assistant to do daily follow-ups. With one particular business partner, both methods helped, getting the DSO down from an average of thirteen days after a job's completion to just two days.

On the flip side, I also recommend looking at payables and all the expenses that can be controlled. You will find that there are some items that can be controlled. For example, most bills allow for a grace period, when you can push back the bill payment for a few days without any additional cost in the form of penalties, relationships, etc. These extra days are valuable when trying to control the flow of money leaving the company. For example, no one should move payroll, since your employees run the business of their households and depend on their pay after performing work. However, paying rent for a business space, like a mortgage, has a few days of leeway before additional costs kick in. You can move bills like this to be paid at the absolute last minute. It makes all the difference in making payroll and controlling your cash inputs and outputs.

I also recommend building a reserve account. A lot of businesses I work with do not have one in place. The rule I recommend is putting a specific percentage of the profit dollars in the reserve account. This helps the business tremendously with free cash flow and an ability to ensure emergencies can be handled.

The cognitive dissonance comes in when people are simply comfortable doing the same tasks, in the same way, over and over, pointing the finger for problems somewhere else. But data can be used to measure and identify the issues and make the necessary positive changes.

Another way to take entrepreneurs beyond the status quo is using silent business partners. These partners have a voice in what is going on in the business, which gives the entrepreneur an added level of accountability. Most entrepreneurs don't have a level of accountability and don't really want one. To enact change, they need to trust those they spend time with and have mentors who have their best interests at heart. It is often a big leap for entrepreneurs to go from doing it all to trusting others to do things as well.

Attacking Cognitive Dissonance

To attack cognitive dissonance and alter the behaviors resistant to change, first recognize that you have some form of cognitive dissonance. You may not be able to do this on your own. One of my most successful tactics when working with business leaders is spending time setting up their meetings and cadences. I then attend those meetings and run them. In three to four weeks, I turn them over to the business leader to run, spending time with them after each meeting in a debriefing session, giving them direct feedback on what they did well to encourage those behaviors and what didn't go so well. I accompany the things that didn't go so well with a recommended change and explain why the change is necessary.

For example, one of my business partners ran his meetings well, but he was mechanical. I worked on teaching him to be an inspirational leader through his word choices, inflections, and the elimination of microaggressions. For example, his approach sounded much like this, "You need to be on time. I don't know why people would even think about not being on time unless they don't care." Instead, I made a link to why they needed to be on time. His words were not inspiring anyone. The change went more like this: "I need everyone to focus on being on time because when we do this, we can get to our customers sooner rather than later. It shows respect to everyone, as one of our values of reliability." The message was the same, but the words were different, and this is the part where leadership style matters.

It takes a long time to change people and how they communicate. It requires lots of training and coaching. Many business leaders resist, thinking that this is the way they always did it. In some cases, I found that the more "blue collar" trades did not want words to be frilly or flowery. And they are right to some extent. They don't have to have flowery language, but they do have to inspire people. People need to know why they are doing something. Business leaders should aim to inspire employees to be like them and be with them in their organization, reminding team members what they get when the overall organization is successful.

Chapter 10:

FEAR OF LOSING CONTROL

Entrepreneurs often find themselves on the road to failure because they fear losing control of the business they are building. Fear of losing control can be a huge stumbling block for nearly everyone, and entrepreneurs may fear losing control more than most. Ultimately, fear of losing control makes people feel vulnerable, so this fear often arises from a lack of trust.

For an entrepreneur specifically, this fear can be grounded in the belief that no one can do the job the way they can. It can also stem from a fear that someone might take advantage of them and use what they have heard, learned, or seen to their own advantage. Entrepreneurs believe that if they aren't in control, it must mean someone else is. After all, the big plus to entrepreneurship is being in control. Being in control is safe and comfortable, but it prohibits growth. Stepping outside of the comfortable, putting strategies in place to ensure standards of work are upheld, trusting the right people, and being disciplined enough to stay on plan are things that help entrepreneurs and their companies grow.

The Root of the Fear of Losing Control

Most entrepreneurs fear losing control of their company to other entities—in most cases investors or employees. Let's explore this concept in more detail.

Entrepreneurs are most often fearful of losing control to investors. Nearly every entrepreneur needs capital at some point, but they want capital their way, on their terms. The fact is, when making large deals with investors, entrepreneurs do have to give up some measure of control. It is difficult to face—and even harder to do. On the positive side, with the right investors, entrepreneurs can leverage the capabilities that the investors bring to the table without losing a great deal of control. Deals with investors don't have to result in loss of control; they can be structured in ways that work with the entrepreneur's role and leverage the knowledge of savvy investors to bring in the right people to grow a strong, successful company.

The other main area of fear of losing control is entrepreneurs fearing the loss of control to employees. This is often the reason why entrepreneurs try to fill all the roles themselves and keep their hand in every aspect of their business. It is a habit that results in entrepreneurs driving themselves crazy because they are simply doing too much.

For example, I looked at one of my business partner's organization via an ordinary organizational chart. His assignment was to color-code the jobs he was doing versus the jobs his employees were doing. We then discussed how he interacted with customers and developed a flowchart of how money flowed through the organization to show everyone's involvement in the business. He was surprised to see he wasn't separating himself from the duties his employees should be handling.

Fear of Losing Control is About Status

Fear of losing control is all about status. I have read about people who are motivated by fear, status, and greed. Thus, fear of losing control crosses the chasm of both fear and status. We all want to be validated for our ability to be the best at what we do. We want the world and, more importantly, those close to us to see us as successful. It's natural to want that. I have worked with leaders who present plans that create a very rosy picture of the future. They should do so, but the assumptions, data points, scenarios, etc. should help them realize that when they have planned in the past, they never got to the rosy future. I usually find that this is because it is very hard to be vulnerable. It is akin to when someone lies to their spouse or partner, knowing that it's not the right thing to do, but fear losing the status they have with their partner. It's the same in business. We must be willing to create best-case scenarios but let the data tell us where we are so that we can develop plans to overcome some of the ugly truths and move toward the rosy picture. The data always tells a story. Let's not ignore it.

For many business partners, I perform an activity in which we look at what was initially planned for the income and costs versus the actuals from the income and costs so that I see can trends. For all business partners, I like to be 80 percent accurate when it comes to income and costs. However, I find that costs are always more accurate in plans than income. It makes sense; there are always fixed costs month to month. These costs may be thrown off by decisions about payment due dates, something that can be controlled in some cases. In one case, I noted that the leader was just too optimistic in the income side, often scoring well below the 80 percent predictability. With this client, here are some additional facts we uncovered:

- The time needed to finish the job and collect the money was always at least seven to ten days longer than planned. The cause was rooted in being overly optimistic and not having a plan for the collection of funds or how the resources would be used.
- There were unforeseen customer change orders. When the customer provided the change order, rather than paying for what was already done, the change order was put in and the invoice

was created. But the due date for the original bill was extended. The business was highly dependent on this money to keep the cash flow positive. The thought process was that it would be a larger payoff all at once, but having the cash today and rules for getting your money now is more beneficial to the business.

- The business did not have a good cash collection mechanism in place because the owner wanted to control cash collection and control the relationship with the customer. This mistrust was very costly to the business, and it took months to make the right change after continuously failing to keep a positive bank balance due to negative cash flow (money going out faster than money coming in).

Entrepreneur's fear losing control of "their baby." Think about it. Entrepreneurs often must go to investors like venture capitalists who may want to control at least 51 percent of the company. It is rare to get a large infusion of capital while allowing the entrepreneur to remain in control. For this reason, many entrepreneurs refuse venture capital funding. But the venture capitalist group has experience growing companies, and if they see you have something valuable, I always say that 49 percent of millions is better than 100 percent of nothing.

It is hard for a human to see their creation converted into something different than their original vision, even when they are still trying to figure out how to get the personal vision they had for themselves and the company. I try to teach business leaders and aspiring entrepreneurs how to create the whole vision and keep that vision, even if they work with a venture capital group. If you are attractive enough (have a good product or service), a venture capital group will let you have some level of control in the shared outcome, but if they see you are not the person for the job, they will move you out and take control.

Fear of losing control can be avoided or overcome through small steps of giving bits and pieces of control when it comes to the less risky items like cash collection. If you have an employee or a business partner, they can collect the cash or provide customer service to your satisfaction. If you don't trust that person, then they are not the right person for your business. Entrepreneurs must realize that if they want to grow, they must rid themselves of the fear of losing control. I often ask, "Do you really want to grow, or do you only want status?" Some just want status without doing what it takes to grow, but you must lose the fear of losing control in order to grow.

Moving Forward without Fear

As we move forward and talk about organizing your business for success, I want to emphasize that it is crucial to delegate responsibilities to get more done. Entrepreneurs must drop the fear of losing control to investors or employees and hire people they can trust. It is true that in doing so they give up some level of control, but the result is the ability to focus on areas they need to control to grow the business. If not, they wind up going back to doing a job rather than running a company.

Many entrepreneurs who find themselves struggling are advised by well-meaning friends, colleagues, and even family members (especially those who have been asked for money to help with the business) to give up the business and get a "real job." A "real job" is simply the comfort zone for most people, but it isn't what entrepreneurs want to do with their life. Everyone is not built to punch a clock, work within the walls of a building, or work for someone else. Entrepreneurs aren't looking to go backward. They are looking to go forward, toward their prize of realizing their dreams. The problem is that most are struggling with the challenges of transitioning from a day-to-day job to being a leader and running a growing business. Therein is the foundation of the RFE: to help entrepreneurs grow in the leader space by understanding the two key components of business—employees and cash flow—and putting the plans and accountability in place to realize their visions!

PART 2:
The Remedies

Entrepreneurs must organize their business for success by developing a project management mindset that allows them to plan, build, divide, and conquer. This mindset helps entrepreneurs create a path to success after their overall goal has been clearly defined and articulated. With it, you can build a solid business case and a set of milestones to help bridge the gap between your current state and where you want to be. You must have this mindset to build a solid team and support that team to deliver the agreed-upon goals. You must have the capability to manage people with multiple roles in the right order to have them working at their optimum efficiency. You must keep them focused on the goal but also recognize that change is the one constant in this world, and you must have the ability to cope with this change. Finally, you and the team must have an unwavering belief that the actual goals can be met.

To delve further into this mindset, there must be the underlying processes that includes selecting the right people to be part of your team. This means not just your employees, but everyone who is part of your business ecosystem: investors, advisors, well-connected colleagues, mentors, etc. Your resources must be able to bring at least one of the following to your business:

- Experience
- Energy
- Cash/Capital
- Time
- People (employees, advisors, customers, and partners).

With these resources, entrepreneurs can organize for success, develop a plan of assessment, build and unite the team, advance change management, and enhance communication to initiate the RFE and grow their business successfully.

Chapter 11:

ORGANIZE FOR SUCCESS

The process of organizing for success begins with stating your goals and articulating the vision for the company. The vision must be stated in a manner that is understandable for everyone, including interested investors and potential customers, and can build excitement among employees. Now the question is: How do we organize and close the gap?

The Process

The process to organize begins with a gap analysis. First, you have the vision. The vision begins with what you want to be and where you want to go, which requires clarity. For example, if you want to have a $5 million-company this year, and that is twice the amount of money you have brought in before, where do you begin?

We begin by looking back. What does $5 million look like? We look at your performance over the past few years to make sure your percentages line up. Your percentage is calculated by taking your income in the past (in this example, let's say it was $2 million) and dividing it by the cost of goods sold as a percentage of sales, gross margin percentage, and your expenses that supported the company at $2 million. These trends help us understand how you are currently operating. We also look at what made up that $2 million. Was there one customer who was 80 percent of your total revenue? What was unique about that customer? This will give us some insight into how we have behaved in the past and what changes may be needed for the future. Finally, we look at the $5 million and break it down to quarterly ($1.25 million), monthly ($417,000), weekly ($96,000) and daily sales ($14,000). Now these figures count every day of the year, so think of these as directional. You can remove the weekends from the equation, but I am willing to bet that if you are running a small business, you are working on weekends. I want you to stop having to work on the weekends! We then align your top line with the percentages we determined from your past to help us create an income statement that shows what the cost of goods sold would be as a percentage of sales, the cost of sales and general administration costs (SGA), and expenses—all as a percentage based on what was performed in the past. Of course, this does not include the scale that is achieved with growth, and I know many leaders who have run large companies will criticize this, but this is my process until it's refined with scale.

Next, we look at all the expenses so we can line up your company behaviors with the percentages that make your company a good company. If you are a construction management company or an IT company, your cost of goods sold or your expenses should be near the average percentages in your industry, and we line those up to check whether we are moving in the right direction. There will be research required to understand this, but that education is valuable to a business owner, who should always know how they are benchmarking in the industry.

Then we answer the question: "What does your organization look like?" Generally, in building to a larger business, we include additional expenditures for new employees. For your company, you may need to hire a project manager, an office manager, and a salesperson or maybe two.

We look at the both the cost of goods sold for additional direct labor and look at what is needed for indirect labor. For this example, growing from $2 million to $5 million is not a big jump. There may be more employees needed for direct labor to support the sales, or we may need to add office personnel or salespeople to support the growing number of customers.

We decide who to hire first by creating two organizational charts: today's organizational chart and tomorrow's organizational chart. In terms of benchmarking, we also compare our organizational chart to larger, more successful companies' organizational charts. For most successful companies, you can find these online. If you want to behave like a certain company, you can see the roles and responsibilities that need to be put in place. You can easily envision what the future state looks like. It may mean acquiring five new people, and this is what we would put in place for your company.

After learning how we need to organize to grow from $2 million to $5 million, we create a budget. Again, many of the expenses may be the same. Perhaps you can stay in the same building and prevent additional costs for space; however, the mobile phone bill might go up. So we review the expenses and develop an overall budget for the business. Yes, I said budget. I am so amazed when I work with entrepreneurs who do not have a budget. When I say you must have a project management mindset, one of the guardrails of project management is cost (budget). This helps you stay grounded in how you manage spending.

As implied in the above dissection, there are two parts of organizing for success: the finances and the people. Now, let's dive a bit deeper, beginning with the people. In our organizational chart, we developed a plan based on where we want to go. To establish the vision and build the chart, we retrieved examples from other companies that look like the company you hope to become. So now that we have the chart, we focus on the roles and responsibilities and be clear on the segregation of duties. Remember, many entrepreneurs are fulfilling many roles. The goal is to get them to fulfill only the role that gets the most out of their talents and focuses on building the business. During the organizational chart exercise, we color-code the boxes on the chart by who is filling those roles, and, often, the leader's color fills way more boxes than it should. In many cases, the client is doing all the business development, marketing, human resources, operations, accounting, finance, investing, community affairs, logistics, treasury, purchasing, billing, and more. To correct this, we must look at how we want the company to be organized.

We want to position the business so that the leader is only handling one or two boxes on the organizational chart. The top box should be the leader of the organization. Next come the people we need to hire, whether that means direct hiring or partnering with a third-party organization to accomplish the necessary duties. It is possible to do a hybrid of both direct hires and third-party contractors, depending on the current cash flow. The idea is to organize the future organization and develop a plan with prioritized hiring as the business grows. Even before we do any new hiring, we look at the people in the current organization and see where they are to determine if we can upskill them and grow them into a certain position. Often there are opportunities to combine positions or upskill rather than going outside the organization, and it is important to let everyone in the organization know what we are hoping to do. Growth and opportunity are exciting for the team. When they see the goals, they often want the new positions and will work to get them.

One exercise I ran with business partners was simply talking through the priority. I knew what the priority should be, but I did not want to inject my thoughts. The idea needed to be their own. I merely facilitated the discussion with the business partners and had them walk through their resource needs multiple times to discover the priority on their own—well, with my guidance. I was incredibly pleased with their outcome. With the leaders, we put a plan in place that took us from where we are today to where we need to be, determining the order we need to hire individuals to meet our goals. We refreshed the budget to make sure it matched the resources needed for the business to meet the goals of the organization.

The second part of organizing for success is organizing financials. It is critical to present the financials clearly, with a chart of accounts that is easy to understand and that shows the company's progress year over year, quarter over quarter. It is also crucial that leaders can interpret what those financials are saying about the company. In most cases, this means hiring an accountant who helps develop a balance sheet, an income statement, and a cash flow statement, delivering key financial ratios that help a company determine its position and what needs to be done to ensure the company stays on track with growth and goals. In addition, a statement of cash flow and a cash forecast enables the company to measure all these factors while looking to the future. Not having these basic items in place can be a huge impediment to raising funds, understanding leakages in finances, and understanding how much they would really need should a bridge loan or capital injection be required to support an opportunity.

In addition to the basic accounting required for businesses, I work with clients to determine the key measures that show whether there is a potential or actual problem. One measure I've already mentioned is a simple success measure of daily, weekly, and monthly sales. If we made a goal to get to $5 million in one year, and we calculated daily sales would need to be around $14,000, the dashboard will clearly show the daily sales, and adjustments can be made. This is never a linear process, but it is intended to inspire action toward the goals. I even created a CEO Dashboard for my business partners to help them manage these financial factors and other key measures of success, including financial measures, employee measures, and customer measures. Seeing where they are going on a regular basis can supplement organizing for success.

Together, organized people and organized financials are poised for success, and that allows leaders to grow their businesses. In short, organizing for success is establishing what the company needs to operate like the company it aspires to be.

There is one final, critical piece to the puzzle: people who are not employees of the company but can still have a critical role in the success of the business. In the same vein that project managers use steering committees with the executives of the company or sponsors who are invested in the project outcomes, business leaders need accountability. And people create accountability. The importance of having accountability partners cannot be discounted. My recommendation is for entrepreneurs to have a board of advisors to keep them accountable, as well as uncomfortable (to the point that they ensure everything is right as they fight through the issues). The accountability group or board of advisors should include members who are well-qualified, experienced in finance/accounting, familiar with the industry, and in a commercial space of marketing that helps to grow the business. Additional leaders can include legal, human resources, and financial advisors. This core group is paramount to ensuring well-rounded accountability, which can help the company grow. With my business partners, I initially serve as the chair of this group to help them build a successful advisory board through my organized approach, helping them understand the RFE so they can continue moving forward.

Build in Milestones

After organization—with clear roles, responsibilities, and metrics—we build in milestones. A milestone has been defined as a marker to indicate distance, an important event such as turning a certain age, or any reference point that marks a critical decision point. Milestones are extremely helpful for showing our progress toward an end goal. My clients perform a prioritization exercise to determine the most important person to hire first. If we determined five resources were needed, we decide who of those five is the priority hire. The number-one resource will be hired when we reach the first milestone income level or business level, because the new hire will need to control new things. We build the job description, get the company ready, and then move forward when we reach the milestone. We do the same for each position, so that's why I say organizing for success is understanding who and what you need (roles, responsibilities, cadence) and how we can work together. This example outlines people milestones, but along with the key measure we put in place, we can create additional milestones. For example, I mentioned that I like for the cash flow exercise to get to 80 percent predictability for income and expenses. We could set the milestone so that by the end of the quarter, we are at 50 percent, the next quarter's milestone could be 65 percent, and the following quarter at 85 percent, which is even slightly above the goal.

With all the moving pieces that come with organizing for success, we must create a way to keep everyone informed of the progress. This comes in the form of change management, a particularly important step to ensure we are managing each level of the organization in a structured way. In my experience with managing projects and working with business partners I've found that most failures in meeting expectations, goals, and relationships stem from someone failing to effectively communicate. I develop a solid change management plan with my clients that includes how we will communicate, a good training plan, and a process for how we walk the milestones together.

True Visionnaires can see themselves in the future, accomplishing goals with the organization. They can then leverage the RFE and walk through the milestones. That's how we organize for success.

An Example of Being Organized for Success

For example, I was once at a company where we spent time developing our sales and operations plan. This was a weekly exercise that I learned with the CEO of the company. We planned for all the garments to be produced in the coming week based on the orders that we received or orders that were not yet filled. We planned everything from the material, the thread, the zippers, etc. This was my first foray into the LEAN principles and planning made-to-order manufacturing. The plan produced a glimpse into the future for the revenue we expected after completing each planned garment with a high degree of quality ready for shipment. Each person had a role to execute this plan, but the person most responsible was the director of operations. As long as he was there to drive the execution of the plan, I could focus on my studies, which included analyzing the costs to make every garment and presenting that cost to the leadership to determine whether the prices needed to be raised.

One day, the director of operations and the senior leaders were not in the office due to several emergencies. We had a situation in the manufacturing operation where we ran short of material and a piece of equipment broke down, so I called the CEO and said, "I don't know what to do."

The CEO responded, "Yes, you do."

I answered, "No, I don't. What do you mean?"

He remarked, "Yes, we already developed a sales and operations plan. Just put the line in that brings in the most money."

It blew my mind because I had no idea that I was already prepared. But it was because we had the right people and had an organization plan in place. We exercised this plan on a weekly basis and adjusted it daily. Planning mattered. Having steps in place to handle a crisis and take us from point A to point B is an intended outcome of organizing for success. Also, knowing the roles of each person who was part of the plan allowed me to be successful adjusting and driving the business in the same manner the CEO would have. We were okay because we were organized for success.

Chapter 12:

DEVELOP A PLAN OF ASSESSMENT

The process continues with developing a plan of assessment combined with a handful of plausible, alternative futures that can be used throughout an entrepreneur's journey to success. Developing a plan of assessment is the key to scenario planning.

When creating a plan of assessment, the first priority for entrepreneurs is to separate the business from the personal. The business plan of assessment examines the strengths and weaknesses of the business. A business assessment can be simple or complex, often dependent on the current size of the business. A smaller, one-man operation will need a simpler assessment than it will when it grows, at which point the assessment will become more complex.

There are tools and techniques that can be used to help with long-term planning and unforeseen changes, as well as to analyze where you currently are. For the long-term, using scenario planning is my preferred method for determining the impact and predictability of an uncertain future.

Many businesses did not look ahead at the devastating impact a pandemic might have, but what if a business had planned for the worst-case scenario and was able to enact that plan to keep their business viable? Scenario planning is not strategic planning, but it is used prior to strategic planning. Scenario planning looks at external situations that could have an impact on your business using the STEEP model (Societal, Technological, Environmental, Economic, Political) of forces that could have a positive or negative impact on your business.

Examining the SWOT Analysis as an Individual

I personally don't subscribe to the SWOT (Strengths, Weaknesses, Opportunities, and Threats) analysis process for businesses. I believe that the information from the process doesn't drive action; it's just a subjective report card. That being said, at the individual level, I believe it is very beneficial. I've done the SWOT analysis many times, particularly when assessing how I can leverage more of my strengths and opportunities. I don't focus as much on my weaknesses as I believe I get more from being stronger at what I am good at. Below is the outcome of my latest self-performed SWOT analysis.

My strengths were:

- Reputation at work
- Collegial
- Exceptional foresight
- Great communicator
- Focused
- Disciplined
- Great role model

My weaknesses were not unique, but it was revealing after I really thought about what keeps me from reaching my full potential. The first was procrastination, which negatively impacts my focus and discipline. This is an example of how a strength can sometimes be a weakness as I had to learn to focus on less. Inconsistency was also a weakness for me in my relationships, which is why I had to develop consistency. You must be consistent to succeed in business and in life.

My desire to invest in others was my biggest weakness. Why? I am a giver, and I always want to help. I would invest in others, with both my money and my time, who didn't want to invest in themselves. I had to learn to make hard decisions and let go when someone doesn't want to achieve their vision more than I do.

For example, I recently had dinner with someone who wanted to be in the car dealership business. I told them to talk to me about it, asking questions about what they needed. I get very excited when someone is talking about their dreams and want to help. I want to dive right in—go to the whiteboard and plan it out. So, I asked, "What is keeping you from starting this business?" He replied that he needed a business plan. I asked, "Why do you need a business plan? What will you use it for? Is it to raise money? Help you as a guide to start your business? Tell me, why is the only impediment a business plan?"

He continued to insist he needed a business plan.

I said, "Well, let's talk about that business plan." As I pressed on, I noticed that he was getting a bit uncomfortable about discussing the business and the business plan. What I should have done right there was leave it alone, but I thought all I had to do was figure out the barriers and he would magically build his business with my help.

However, after asking a series of questions, I built a simple five-step business plan and offered it to him, telling him, "Here is your business plan. You have already accomplished number one, as you have already enrolled in a class to get certified in the business. It's already paid for, so that is a sunk cost. Go ahead. Take the class and earn the certification. Number two is that you stated you have relationships with three or four people who can help you get the cars you need to get started. Your next step is to call them and ask if you can do business with them. Start the relationship early to give yourself some leeway. Number three is set your business up, hire an accountant and an attorney, and discuss the type of business structure you need. List the costs involved, and then plan for them. Number four is that as you are working with the contacts to gain contracts, you will need a location for the car dealership. The next action is to look for the location and determine the costs to own or lease the land. Number five is work those contracts with your contacts to get cars and land contracts (owning or leasing)."

I recommended leasing as the least costly option. Then I said, "Now you should be in business in the next few months. This is your plan. It is easy. Five steps, and I can help you with getting started if you want."

When I built this plan for him and sent the email, as well as made a follow-up call, I got no response, which let me know I needed to let this go because I wanted to help him get started in business more than he wanted to get his business started. When I was younger, I would have hounded him as if it were my business because I could see the vision and I wanted to do it, but this was his business, so I had to let it go. It was a weakness that took me a long time to let go of. My strength is taking someone's dream and making it a reality, but it's my weakness when I am pulling someone to satisfy my ego with their dreams when all they wanted to do was talk about it. I jokingly tell my mother that she shouldn't talk to me about what she wants to do unless she really wants to do it—because I am going to make it happen. If she just wants to talk, call my sister or a girlfriend!

As for my opportunities, I looked at the opportunities of the people I worked with back then and the contracts I could get, as well as the threats at the time. The year was 2012, and the threats began with the potential for stimulus funds running out. I was running a business during the period of aid after the financial crisis (2009–2012). It started as an opportunity that I leveraged to start my own business, but it had a short life, and those opportunities began to dry out.

I had polarized thoughts about my direction at the time. I still wasn't clear on my vision, but when I look back at what I had then—five income streams of investments, real estate, business ownership, freelance work, and consulting—life was not as bad as I thought.

When I look at where I am now, I have learned a great deal that helped me grow in each of those areas. Now I have two separate businesses, and while my freelance work has not increased, I still do management consulting and teaching, which is what I was ultimately was born to do.

SWOT analysis works very well on an individual level, but too many factors are involved in business for it to work well. I have done SWOT analyses with businesses, but the analysis is too static to provide sound guidance. My guide for a plan of assessment is to perform a risk assessment with a STEEP model.

Let me first define the difference between an issue and a risk. An issue is something that already happened, something you need to deal with. A risk is something that has the potential to happen, and there must be a plan to mitigate the risk. We will do a risk management exercise to help identify the specific risks and issues with growing the business. The risk management exercise addresses the items that are currently in the way. The risk is given a title to briefly describe it, an explanation of why addressing it is necessary, the action plan to resolve it, highlights of any dependencies that must be resolved in order to mitigate the risk, and finally who is responsible for resolving the risk and their due date. You can get a little deeper with this assessment by providing information on the probability that the risk will occur and its impact with a score of high, medium, or low. This is part of a project manager's must-have toolkit as the risks can be roadblocks that keep you from realizing your vision. They come in various forms, and, in some cases, you may not even know how to identify a risk.

One exercise I like to perform with an entire team is to have them list all the reasons that something might fail. I ask this when discussing the outcomes of a specific project or the goals that we are trying to achieve because I get a diverse look at what people are thinking or seeing and the insight is tremendous. This builds the baseline risk management plan.

Clearing the Fog: Risk assessment and mitigation
Finances and proper financial processes are the key risk factors impeding growth for BDFS

Risk #	Risk title	Why Necessary	Actions/Dependency	Status
1	People: Lack of organization for success	Having an organized group to focus on business development and operations is key. 2 people run the entire organization	Hire 4 key roles in 2021	Not Started
2	Finances: Complicated bank account structure	Building an easy way to follow cash-inflows and outflows.	Agreement by Co-Founders	Completed on 12/27
3	Finances: No clear standard for estimates/pricing based on labor & material costs	Predictability of income is key to success and prevents any income loss that may occur from underpricing. Also, to hire an estimator in the future requires a standard to be developed.	Need Calvin to develop this by Jun 2021. Calvin will begin using Builders Trend and iPower to help with this	Not Started
4	Finances: Lack of financial reserves	Fund the reserve account: Need a safety net to keep the business viable – learned that this is crucial with the pandemic and impact of losing a large contract through the behaviors of the client	Need to establish the process and execute	Completed on 12/27
5	Finances: No clear process to capture cash immediately after completion of work	Too much of Calvin's time is spent in collections. This is the lifeline of all business. Not enough emphasis is placed on this	Calvin needs to relinquish this role to another. Hiring the controller will help.	Not Started
6	Finances: Lack of capital for growth	In order to capture and support very large commercial projects, BDFS requires access to capital for mobilization.	Target for $100K with investors or bank lines of credit. Debt needs to be significantly reduced in order to make this happen	Not Started
7	Finances: Large debt impeding growth opportunities	Over $200K in (bad) debt makes BDFS unattractive for investors and partners. In order to grow through acquisition or organically, we need to eliminate this to under $50K – unless debt (good debt) is used for leverage (growth)	Need to develop and execute a debt reduction plan that starts in January and is restructured by July 2021	Not Started

The STEEP Model for Business

Just the like the risk management plan, the STEEP model is used to determine the major implications of what *could* get in the way and how we would react. This takes risk management a little deeper and requires some higher-level thinking. I've liked using this analysis since I first learned of its effectiveness in a strategy class back in 2007. The five elements of STEEP include: Social, Technological, Economic, Ecological, and Political (Legal). STEEP is an amazingly effective analytical tool, particularly during times of uncertainty. The year 2020 was definitely a time of uncertainty, and businesses should look at the pandemic, along with the 2008 financial crisis and the 2001 attacks on the world trade center, as examples of anomalies that could devastate their business. They must determine a game plan they can employ should it happen. No one can predict the future, but you can plan for devastating events. Just like you buy insurance to help you in those times, consider the planning as a form of insurance.

Let's look at each of the elements of STEEP.

The social impact is a crucial factor for most business, especially during the closures and uncertainty surrounding the global pandemic. As I work with teams to build their fiscal plans for the new year, we now include preparation for additional lockdowns. This makes it critical to focus on capturing as much cash as possible, because cash can get the business through another lockdown (or similar situation) successfully.

The next factor, technology, is continually evolving, making it a factor in every business. The question I ask my clients here is, "Which of the anticipated changes in technology can affect your business?" Some businesses will not have major technological impacts, but others (technology-driven industries) will, and it can be a threat for them. I like to look at it and ask, "If this technological situation occurs, what will you do? How will you respond?" One thing that comes to mind is 3-D printing. If you are currently in the business of building houses, how will you compete against the trend of people going to cheaper and faster options like 3-D printing?

Another factor is economic conditions. Economic conditions can seem like they are very good, but they change constantly, so the question is, "What changes might occur in the economy that could impact your business? If you think about the number of unemployed people, you may be able to hire well-qualified individuals who are available. But in other circumstances, those same individuals may not be available. So, what happens when you need to hire qualified individuals but wages are going up because the demand is higher for resources? You must consider changes in the economy so that you can be prepared for both a downturn (less people buying your product) or a boom (higher demand, creating higher costs for you to serve your customers).

The next factor is environmental. Climate change is in the news nearly every day. As climate changes can affect every aspect of life and work, we are having longer summers and shorter winters. These conditions directly impact your company if your business is dependent on weather. For example, if the winters are so harsh that you can't do your work (construction, landscaping, etc.), this leads back to the importance of managing cash flow. You have to know how you will pivot if, in the winter months, your company cannot garner new business.

For one client, I asked, "How do you smooth out the business?" Most of his business came in the winter, and he had bad summer months based on the contracts he had. If he had a harsh winter and was unable to work and then didn't have a good summer, it was bad. I helped him plan for good and bad summers, in terms of weather and his business. Our focus was to create business contracts to be delivered during the summer. It was not easy, but seeing his income profile, we knew where we had to do the most work.

The last element is political/legal. The political environment can hurt or help your company based on taxes. Some years there are politicians who want to tax businesses more, and others want to tax businesses less. As a business owner, you must determine the set-asides or programs different political leadership allows you, as well as how you structure your company. You may want to be an S corporation in certain political arenas and a C corporation or LLC in others. I go through this with business partners asking, "What could possibly happen? What couldn't possibly happen? What is likely? If this happens, how will you respond?" Each one, when using the STEEP analysis, has a set of actions already in place depending on the circumstances of that year.

Going back to the scenario in which the CEO wasn't available and someone else was left in charge, when someone asked what they need to do, they should always be able to go back to the plan. The plan and the assessment help clear the fog and prepare you. You can go into battle with all your tools and weapons, and you are ready to take action. When you watch the news, you can look and listen for clues to help you pivot your business in the right direction. With a plan, you can reach your numbers and clear the fog.

Even with a plan in place from the STEEP analysis, a basic business assessment should also include positives (successes) and negatives (areas for improvement). There should also be a section for goals not yet met, current challenges, and any setbacks that have occurred since the last assessment. Finally, it should contain ideas for how to address the setbacks in positive, growth-oriented ways.

Strategy Implications – Scenario Planning
What moves will we need to make if certain scenarios play out

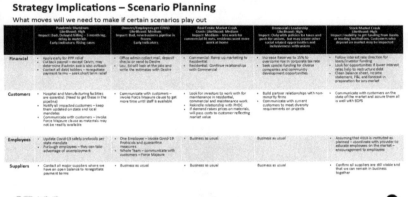

Chapter 13:

ORGANIZE THE TEAM

As part of the process, entrepreneurs must develop strong relationships with their team members and organize their team to handle any additional work that comes from growth. It is also wise to have a pool of potential talent to draw from when the need arises.

Building and organizing a high-performing team is the key to day-to-day operational success. At first, the team may be small. It also may include paid professionals or advisors outside the business, including marketing professionals, an accountant or bookkeeper, an attorney, a banker, etc. As the business grows, paid professionals or advisors in positions such as attorneys, bankers, and the like may remain.

For your core team, the right resources for successful day-to-day basic operation include:

- Office Manager: takes inbound calls, makes calls on the business's behalf, manages customer service, social media marketing, accounts receivable, accounts payable (Note: These duties are now easily performed by virtual assistants.)
- Sales Manager: builds the sales plan, manages sales team, executes sales strategy

- Project Manager/Director: manages the employees who touch customers, helps build strategy, executes the projects that meet the company's vision
- Operations Manager/Director: ensures day-to-day operations are happening, responsible for sales and operations plans and execution.

Additional team members can be added as growth occurs, including accountant, bookkeeper, marketing professionals, etc.

The resources in the list above are foundational positions in any company. These are positions often filled by the business owner or a few people performing all the responsibilities. Your goal is to grow your business enough to have these positions—and more—with specific duties that move the company in the direction of its stated vision and mission. Keep in mind, there are two fundamental parts to every business: operations (ongoing) and projects (temporary endeavors). Even so, to be a viable company you must make money; therefore, a sales infrastructure must be considered if you plan to really grow. There are many businesses that sell in any number of ways, but when your business relies on customers who must be attracted and converted, by methods other than the internet, a sales team with a sales manager is crucial for major growth. In addition to growing sales, which also means that you have more risk opportunities, having individuals who can help you with compliance and guide you in minimizing risk to your business is also critical. This is where accountants and lawyers are key.

Building a board of directors will be valuable as well. The late Jack Welch summarized that the most important decisions you will ever make are who you hire and who you fire. I suggest the people with whom you surround yourself is an equally important decision. The right people can save you hundreds, even thousands, of dollars.

When I talk to many entrepreneurs about going from their vision to reality, I explain that follow-through is the place between the vision and the reality. Follow-through is the most important part of the process, which is why I work with entrepreneurs to develop all the steps, in digestible pieces, that can be executed during the follow-through.

Remember, what is in your mind (the vision) is not real. It can only be made real during the follow-through. Entrepreneurs must open their minds and understand that the process is not easy, but it is simple: focus on what you want!

Think about the business in terms of size and dollars. Focus on understanding the financials and connecting with the humans in your ecosystem to organize a great team of people who report directly to you.

On top of that, you need to develop your own accountability system—a group of individuals who can act as a board of advisors for you. This group should include your attorney and your accountant, as well as trusted mentors who have succeeded in your industry. Listen to them, and then get out of your own way. Keep in mind, you didn't go to school for accounting (in most cases), you didn't go to school for project management, and you didn't go to law school, so open up to working with these individuals to achieve the growth and success you envision. Spend time learning the process, understanding the steps, letting go, and allowing your team of professionals help with growth and success. It will happen for you if you allow it to!

Building Relationships

Every businessperson, regardless of industry, has relationships that are either transactional or strategic. A strategic relationship is one that has your best interests at heart; you are comingled with the entity you have a relationship with. A transactional relationship is usually a one-and-done, mutually agreed-upon act that may or may not contribute to the overall vision but is a necessary thing for your business.

For example, a transactional relationship with the bank is one in which you put money in the bank, take money out, apply for loans, are accepted or rejected, and pay loans back, but no one really knows you because every time you go there is a different person you do business with. A strategic relationship with the bank is one in which the banker or bank officials knows who you are and what your business does and are eager to support your business's banking needs. When you go in with your specific needs, the banker wants to work out some plans for the future. In this relationship, the banker is helping you solve your problem, and, in doing so, they benefit as well. You want to build a strategic relationship with the bank so that they offer you the best opportunities for capital when you are seeking to grow your company. Having a person on your advisory board who is also a banker is a bonus.

Transactional Versus Strategic

A transactional relationship versus a strategic relationship is like the similarities and differences between a mentor and a sponsor. A mentor is a trusted advisor in your field or industry. They will always be there to help guide you, provide advice, and maybe even recommend you for a position. Mentorship is a transaction relationship structure in comparison to the strategic relationship that a sponsor can provide. A sponsor is an individual or entity who will stake their reputation on you, backing you and your company emphatically in the business world. The sponsor may even invest in your company. The difference is that while a mentor may make a recommendation for a position or project for you or your company, a sponsor will recommend you or your company, willing to stake their own reputation or finances on you or your company. While both mentors and sponsors are important relationships to build, sponsors are the more strategic relationships—deeper, stronger, and with greater commitment. Strategic relationships with sponsors are the relationships you want to have with all your people, not just transactional relationships—even when the nature of the business itself may be transactional.

Key Relationships

In addition to previous examples, there are some key relationships businesses need for success. If you want to build a better business, you must build better relationships. Relationships are crucial to developing the business you hope to achieve. Scott Galloway, in his talk about the Algebra of Happiness, mentions that one of the key elements is who you choose as a partner. In this case, he is talking about a spouse. This is a crucial element and is one of the most basic of relationships, but it is a key relationship to be successful in life. This also translates to business relationships. I advise my business partners on the importance of building relationships with their employees, customers, professional service providers, and communities. Even in a relationship in which you are paying for goods or services, you might find a window into other businesses that may be able to help you and your business with issues that arise. They may know someone, have seen something, or worked through similar issues. For example, whenever I have a new idea, I like to run it by my financial advisor and ask him about relationships or introductions he might have that can help me clear the fog around what I am hoping to achieve.

Building relationships with your employees is equally important. To do so, you must listen to them and register their feedback. Giving them a voice is part of knowing your people. The voice of your employees is very significant when it comes to helping them feel engaged. An engaged employee is an employee who will stick with you and your company because they feel valued. Keeping open communication with employees is key.

Developing engaging relationships with your customers is also important. We live in a society where social proof is required before people make buying decisions and do business with your company. With all the rankings, ratings, and net promoter scores showcasing the details about you, your company, and your performance, it is crucial that you have strong relationships with your customers because, in turn, they bring in new customers for you and grow your company with their positive reviews. If you get a negative review, attack it head-on. Ask why they left a negative review and remedy the problem quickly. It is your reputation at stake, and you certainly do not want to besmirch your reputation with a lack of response when you could rectify the problem. In some cases, negative reviews result from misunderstandings, but it always important to take the time to respond and build those solid relationships with customers.

I always have my business partners measure their clients' satisfaction. Often the smaller businesses will ask why it is necessary. Client satisfaction tells a story of how the business is performing. It is important not to run from being scored by customers because customers keep businesses going.

Building relationships with the community, joining the local Chamber of Commerce, going to networking events, and becoming a community leader can really help you build a network of exceptional individuals and get your name and brand out there. The fact is that people do business with people they know. I always advise business leaders to spend time meeting new people in areas that allow them to grow their business. It is so important!

Having relationships with the people you do business with regularly is also critical for business success. Banking is one area where I advise business partners to build relationships. Recently I conferred with a client who has worked over a long period to build a strategic relationship with his bank. It took him a few years, and he was in the real estate business. He started with a typical transactional loan, but when he met with loan officer, he showed him the RFE plan, which impressed the banker. Over time, they developed a strong relationship, which has led to an open line of credit in the hundreds of thousands. Now when he walks into the bank and tells them about the deals we are planning to make or projects we are planning to do, the bank gets behind him every time. Why? He has demonstrated his ability to make money and get business, but more importantly, he has demonstrated his ability to make money for the bank.

You need to think about all the relationships you have through the lens of figuring out what is in it for them and how you can help them. I have found that when you go in with this approach, people are ready, willing, and able to help you!

Chapter 14:

CHANGE MANAGEMENT AND COMMUNICATION

I n my experience as a project manager for over twenty years, one of the greatest areas of concern when looking at the lessons learned from a project is communication. I have had some of the most successful projects report low grades in communication. Why is that? How can a project that was deemed widely successful get such scrutiny in the realm of communication?

The answer is that communication is up to individual interpretation. What matters to one person who felt like they received enough communication will not matter to others who require different forms of communication. That is why it is crucial to have many forms of communication on a regular basis. Regular communication on a daily, weekly, monthly, and quarterly basis is a necessity for entrepreneurial business success.

Communication comes in many forms, all of which are important for your business. Let's first talk about customer communications. Realistically building a list of prospects, customers, clients, and referrals all begins with communication. A CRM (Customer Relationship Management) tool is a great starting point from which entrepreneurs can strategically plan touch-points in the form of calls, emails, and even mailers. Leveraging a CRM has many advantages, one of which is electronic and physical mailers. One of my business partners uses mailers to provide discounts for their services, encourage referrals, seek out new employees, and provide useful information for customers (e.g., winter is coming, so make sure you change your air filter) to gain a higher personal touch. In addition to these mailers, they communicate through social media, YouTube videos, customer appreciation outings, etc.

We developed a simple CRM to help keep track of the last time their clients and prospects were last touched through some form of communication. These tools become more sophisticated and easier to set up as technology improves, making integration into your business a less daunting task. A CRM tool can be invaluable when an entrepreneur has their vision and goals in place, as was the case with another client. In this example, the entrepreneur wanted to grow her Mary Kay business. Her vision was to increase the number of team members from ten to one hundred. Mary Kay is a business in which the numbers game must be played, and in order to be successful, you have to talk to and recruit a lot of people.

Her goals were to achieve $150,000 annually per team member of with an overarching goal to create $100,000 in residual income via two streams. The first stream was events and sales, and the second stream was team residuals.

We developed five goals that included:

- Host twelve parties per month for twelve months
- Perform eight facials per month
- Schedule and perform sixty interviews for prospects to join the team per month
- Add fifty new team members by the end of the first quarter and an additional fifty by the end of the second quarter for a total of one hundred new members
- Personal goal: purchase a new or used car (Chevrolet Equinox) eight months after beginning the plan

Once we had the goals, the question became, "How can we do that?" We created a one-page strategy to show the 25 percent residual income per month per team member. The next question was, "How are you going to reach these people?"

And this is when the customer relationship management tool came into play.

For this client, we began with a rudimentary approach—the spreadsheet—avoiding the added expenses of purchasing a CRM like Salesforce. Why a rudimentary approach? I wanted to get her and her team into the practice of actually performing customer relationship management. I had them list prospects—people they knew or they were acquainted with. The idea was to come up with as many names as possible with the goal of putting together a list above and beyond the one-hundred-person goal they had set. After all, in nearly all instances, you are only going to get a small percentage of people to come on board unless you continue building on the list. I had them list first and last names, phone number, and email. Next, they were to classify each individual as a client, a customer, or a prospect.

A client is an individual who consistently buys from you. They are loyal to your business, refer other potential customers, and always have your back. A customer is an individual with whom you have done business, but they are not yet a client because they have not yet provided repeat business. Your goal is to turn your customers into your clients. A prospect is any individual who was referred to you, someone you already know, or a new acquaintance who has not purchased from you yet. You want to prospect them and convert them into a customer first and then a client.

After classifying each individual, we discussed the opportunity level for each. They had a prospect they wanted to turn into a customer, customers they wanted to become clients, and, in this scenario, clients they wanted to convert into team members. Remember, the goal was to get more team members (one hundred of them), as the team members were the ones who provide the most residual income.

We created three columns and asked, "How many times did you touch each person throughout the year?" Touching can be any communication in which you let them know new information about your business or invite them to an event. The next question was, "When was the last time you touched them?" followed by, "When is your next planned touch?" This is a simple marketing plan. Next, we asked, "Are you going to have a big party? Are you going to have a number of people send brochures or discount offers? What is your next touch?"

In this case, we worked together to plan gatherings and subsequently sent out invitations to these events. At this point, I asked my clients to determine a figure known as the "opportunity value." The question is, "How much money do you think you can earn from selling to this person or these collective groups of people?" The opportunity value depends on what you are selling and what you believe you can earn from them. The number created—the opportunity value—was based on seventy-five people with various opportunity levels. The total opportunity came to $177,000, well above the goal of $150,000 they had set. It is crucial to go above and beyond the original goal with the opportunity value since you can never fully predict how much a person will spend.

Next, they measured the actual value when they had touched the customer, asking, "What was the actual value achieved?"

As we begin the analysis, this question arose, "We thought this individual or group would be $7,500 and we only earned $300 from them. What do we need to do, and how do we adjust for that difference?" That leads us to factor in the overall probability, which is a measure of the probability that the individual will do business with them. That probability range is developed by asking a few more questions: "Have they done business with us before?" If they have, that is a higher probability, so we estimate it at 75 to 100 percent. If they are new prospects who have never done business with you, they are estimated at 25 percent because they still need to be converted.

Once everyone on the list is assigned a probability range, a scale can be created based on whether the individual knows us, whether they have done business with us, and whether they are repeat customers.

Additional columns on the spreadsheet include priority. I advised my clients to put a higher priority on those who were clients because they are the bread and butter of the business. They could also put a high priority on a group of prospects if they feel those individuals will help them achieve their goals more quickly.

With all that said, a CRM is basically just a customer relationship management system that allows you to manage information about your clients, customers, and prospects to put yourself in the best position to sell them your products or services. I do it with my business partners at the beginning through a normal, easy spreadsheet until the company grows. After growth, the company can use a CRM system like Salesforce. A custom CRM is so much more robust, allowing you and your company to look at your sales funnel and your sales opportunities, as well as measure your wins and losses. Wins and losses are important to track. Doing so shows whether you are good at converting prospects into clients and, if not, how you need to hone your business acumen and do better.

Creating a vision of sales opportunities in this way also creates excitement among your employees as they see each opportunity by its value. In the case study here, you will see the model for the Mary Kay business using these communication techniques successfully.

Mission:

Goal 1:	Host 12 parties per month for 12 months in 2015
Goal 2:	Perform 8 facials per month
Goal 3:	Schedule and perform 60 interviews for Prospects per month to join my team
Goal 4:	50 new team members by 5/31, additional 50 by 7/31
Goal 5:	Purchase a new or used car by August 1st 2015 - Chevrolet Equinox

Residual % 25%	Monthly Income Per Team Member								
	$100.00	$150.00	$200.00	$250.00	$300.00	$350.00	$400.00	$450.00	$500.00
Team Members	Yearly Totals								
10	$3,000.00	$4,500.00	$6,000.00	$7,500.00	$9,000.00	$10,500.00	$12,000.00	$13,500.00	$15,000.00
30	$9,000.00	$13,500.00	$18,000.00	$22,500.00	$27,000.00	$31,500.00	$36,000.00	$40,500.00	$45,000.00
50	$15,000.00	$22,500.00	$30,000.00	$37,500.00	$45,000.00	$52,500.00	$60,000.00	$67,500.00	$75,000.00
75	$22,500.00	$33,750.00	$45,000.00	$56,250.00	$67,500.00	$78,750.00	$90,000.00	$101,250.00	$112,500.00
100	$30,000.00	$45,000.00	$60,000.00	$75,000.00	$90,000.00	$105,000.00	$120,000.00	$135,000.00	$150,000.00

Strategy: Two streams of income

		Goal	Daily Tasks	Weekly Tasks	Monthly Tasks
Stream 1	Events (Selling)	$40k per year			
Stream 2	Team Residual	$60k per year			

1. Create prospects
1   Selling prospects
2   Team Prospects
2. Develop Team Selling Strategy

= Current Team Members
= Team Members by 5/31
= Team Members by 7/31

									Overall		Sale			Actual	
				Mary Kay Explosion Sales Sheet				$21,000	Probability	50%	Forecast	$10,500.00		sales	$0
First	Last Name	Contact Number	E-mail	Customer Type	Opportunity Type	Touches in 2014	Last Touch	Next Touch	Opportunity Value	Actual Value	Party Scheduled	Guest Night Scheduled	Date Entered	Probability	Priority	Sales Stage	Notes
Janice	Bynum			Prospect	Customer				$1,000				01/01/15	50%			
Ahmed	Kpou			Customer	Team Member				$7,500				01/01/15	50%			
Yvonne	Mullen			Client					$1,000				01/01/15	50%			
Jean	David			Prospect					$1,000				01/01/15	50%			
Colleen	Boyd			Prospect					$1,000				01/01/15	50%			
Bobbie	Alston			Prospect					$1,000				01/01/15	50%			
Amber	Francazio			Prospect					$1,000				01/01/15	50%			
Avonda	Johnson			Prospect					$7,500				01/01/15	50%			

Income and Expenses

Costs	2015											
	January	February	March	April	May	June	July	August	September	October	November	December
Jan. 2 & 3 Mary Kay event, January Jumpstart, Rehobeth beach, DE.												
Jan. 5 first meeting in my home. Business planning for the next 3 months												
Jan. 8 & 9 Mary Kay Parties												
Jan. 10 January Jump with Stacey Harrison in Owings Mill, Md.												
Jan. 12 Meeting/guest night												
Jan. 13,19 & 16 MK party												
Jan. 17-21 MK leadership conference in Nashville TN.												
Jan. 23 & 24 MK parties												
Jan. 26 Meeting/guest night												
Jan. 27 & 29 MK parties												
Jan. 30- Feb. 9 SC, GA, and FL Selling, Booking and recuiting....												
Income												

In addition to creating a great CRM to engage customers, listening is the most important form of communication. Business owners know their business (or their products and services) but can be oblivious to the other voices around them: employees, customers, etc. The best business owners create a platform for others to speak up and help drive solutions. Listening to these groups' thoughts, opinions, and observations will offer a great deal of insight into what is actually happening in the company. For customers, I like to ask my business partners to keep a database or spreadsheet of any complaints. You can use this information to ensure that a trend of specific complaints is resolved or that you don't repeat an issue with another customer. The same spreadsheets can include comments next to the person's name to capture additional details. If you have someone taking inbound calls, have them log every complaint with as much detail as possible to understand the issue voiced by the customer. This can be an invaluable tool to give you information to take action. I also add customer complaints to the dashboard that I create for my business partners so that they can see the number of complaints and take action to resolve them quickly.

Change Management

Communication and listening are also key with your employees, especially when introducing change. Change can occur frequently or not, but it is important that whatever the change, it is properly communicated with the understanding of the expectations of employees when the change is implemented. I like to define change management as not just bringing solutions to the people but bringing the people to the solutions. When you talk about the number of people involved in your company to set your business up for growth, you need to understand everyone's role and responsibility in the change and the impact of the change on employees.

For example, if you want to bring in office automation, your office manager or administrative team whose jobs will be automated may be intimidated if they do not have the technical aptitude for the proposed automation. They may worry that the change will ultimately relieve them of their jobs. You want them to embrace the change and not fight against it, so you must present it as an opportunity for their personal growth as well as that of the company.

If you automate part of the CEO or entrepreneur's duties, like a POS system that would remove the need for the CEO or entrepreneur to collect funds, understanding the impact on all individuals involved is crucial. It is critical to understand the change from the point of view of each person who is affected and work to reassure them you are implementing changes to ensure their time is used for tasks of greater value.

If you take a task away from someone, provide a new task—a growth opportunity, for example—to learn the new technology and teach it to others in the organization. Work to uncover the goals and aspirations of your employees, how they hope to develop and grow. This lends itself directly to listening and communication. A quick way to develop a change management plan is to assess all stakeholders who will be impacted. Create a list of those impacted stakeholders, both internal and external. Then perform an analysis of them. Do they typically embrace change?

Do they freak out whenever they must do something new? Knowing this up-front helps you develop the right type of communication so that you can keep the individual focused on the positive aspects of the change rather than the reasons why the change might not work. Know that when you begin talking to your team, customers, peers, advisors, etc. about your vision for the first time, that is change, and you want to ensure that they get the message clearly and don't create their own assumptions. Building a stakeholder analysis will reveal whether you have the ability to listen and anticipate reactions based on your experience with everyone. Know that in some cases, you won't know. Just like the CRM process helps you as you keep doing it, so will the change management process when you keep engaging in it with your stakeholders.

To summarize change management, you begin with an analysis of all the stakeholders who will be impacted. Next, you develop a plan to get them to adopt the new change, accept the new processes and tools, welcome the new people, and embrace the growth into a bigger, better company.

Listening and Communication

Every entrepreneur should spend time with all their employees, individually and collectively. It is the only way to understand what they want, what is in it for them, what they are hoping to achieve, and what they aspire to become. It is important for you, the entrepreneur, to determine how you can help them achieve their personal goals. When you approach change and communication from this angle, your employees will become almost cult-like in their following of you—because you care about them and their goals.

This is especially true when new leadership comes in to oversee the work and employees feel they have been downgraded from dealing directly with you. The messaging with any change must be clear in letting employees know that they are not being pushed down or out and they are valuable to the company. Explain clearly how you are bringing in a new employee with a significant level of expertise that will add value to their work and income for the company. The current employees gain opportunities as well with things like more training, more travel, more growth, and being part of something larger and better. Creating a vision, and having everyone in the company see and embrace that vision, is an important part of compelling leadership.

Communication and Change Management are Constants

Communication and change management are constant for a successful business. You must build out a communication plan. How will you communicate well on a regular, ongoing basis? One way is to create a weekly meeting to talk about the operation in general, along with separate weekly meetings that allow each employee to speak with their supervisor or manager about ongoing needs. These meetings also provide leadership an opportunity to listen.

In the operations meetings, you should have a few items to review, like sales, business development, financials, cash flow, opportunities, etc. This leads to the ability to prioritize, improve, and communicate. It also allows the team the opportunity to evaluate customer issues and develop remediation plans around customers. In this case, the CEO may have to go and visit a customer. A roundtable discussion is a great approach for these smaller meetings, and in organizations with ten or less employees, they give everyone a voice and allow them to offer areas of improvement. The voices of your employees are tremendous and can be invaluable.

You must create a listening post, where individuals can talk to their supervisors alone, or where they can talk in groups. You, as the leader, must facilitate this, because not every employee is prone to speaking up.

Quarterly meetings should be held with your board of directors or advisors. In these meetings, you can explain what is happening in the company and listen to their advice for how to drive your company to growth. This is particularly important if your board of advisors includes someone who has been in your spot before, a mentor who has grown a similar business.

It is also important not to discount events like happy hours or other get-togethers for employees, which can also fuel communication. Humans are social creatures. What I have found in working with businesses is that when company leadership and employees get together more often in the spirit of accomplishment, there is a greater appreciation for the workplace, as well as the leadership and other team members. These gatherings should always be focused on building solid relationships. I have one client who does this exceptionally well. He takes care of his employees and works to celebrate wins with them. Every year, he schedules a spring mixer for his team members, as well as a holiday party in December. In addition, he plans a summer gathering in Atlantic City for employees and customers to show his appreciation. The goal in gathering should always be expanding touchpoints and enhancing relationships.

In modeling the concept of building relationships with customers and employees, I always recommend spending time together with a purpose. In one instance, the goal of an event was a community-based scholarship award ceremony for other businesses and young entrepreneurs who wrote exceptional essays about why being a business owner is not only beneficial to the individual but to society as a whole.

Another significant gathering point could be for employee recognition. As humans, we all need validation. We want to feel valued, so I always wholeheartedly support organizations that provide employee recognition.

Social gatherings of any kind also work to reduce barriers between business leaders and their employees, which is crucial in the gaining trust of your employees, who carry the mantle and drive the organization forward.

Chapter 15:

MENTAL PREPARATION FOR IMPLEMENTATION

Another important part of the process is mental preparation. Mental preparation begins with the recognition that entrepreneurs never get to the realization of their vision by doing what got them to the point they are currently. This premise finds its foundation in a book by Marshall Goldsmith called *What Got You Here Won't Get You There*. Oftentimes, as humans, we take our initial successes and boast about the great job we did getting to that point and then refuse to refresh our methods to get to the next point.

The business partners I work with and the audience I speak to are business owners who have an established company and have survived the initial five years in which many small businesses die. These entrepreneurs and business owners are operating on a day-to-day basis, but they are not growing. In some cases, they are working payroll to payroll and have developed a sense that this is their normal. They want to grow, but that growth requires mental preparation before they can implement the changes needed to grow. The way they have operated in the past simply will not get them to the growth and success of the future for which they long.

A great deal of the issue they face is self-confidence. While their self-confidence may have been built over years of previous success, it has now plateaued. There are times when self-confidence reaches so great a height that it can make an entrepreneur seem delusional, believing in the success they already achieved so much that they become resistant to implementing the necessary changes for growth and continued success. It is an idea many must fight.

If you are in that place, riding on the high of your previous success, mental preparation for implementation means fighting against the status quo and fighting for change. You must get comfortable with being uncomfortable. Discomfort precedes success. You must change because positive change is in your best interest. You must align your mind with the new vision, whether the alignment you want to see is business growth, enhanced status, a more robust bottom line, or an increase in power, popularity, and money.

If you can't decide the best path for moving forward in mental preparedness for implementation, you should work with someone—be it a mentor, consultant, or another guide—who you trust to help you with this issue. You begin by creating a list of what you should continue to do in your business to take you to the next level, as well as what you must stop doing to succeed. A simple example is that you must stop running all the operations and collecting cash on your own. Another would be that you must stop taking all the customers' calls and delegate that job to someone else, only dealing with customers to get new business, save your reputation, or deal with a severe problem. Get a qualified employee in your organization to do these tasks so you can focus on the areas in which you excel. You might excel at business development, but because you are so involved in day-to-day operations, you have no time to focus there. It is crucial to determine which areas you can delegate to trusted employees and prepare yourself mentally for getting to the next level in business.

Mental preparation for implementation starts with understanding what Tim Ferris so eloquently explained: if you want to have a great quality of life, you need to put together a great team—be it physical or virtual. With your team in place, you must then begin to prepare them to reach your target customers.

When I prepared myself for implementation, I first had to spend time learning about sales and sales processes. Earlier I mentioned using a CRM tool to capture sales prospects, clients, etc. I spent an entire year (2014) learning and practicing sales techniques after signing up for Jack Daly's course and reading his blog. For me to help others, I needed to have my own experience. This was a big paradigm shift for me, and I needed to be mentally prepared for my own growth. I practiced this on myself, and I have now worked with so many other clients to develop their sales acumen and take their mindsets from "I am not a salesperson" to understanding that sales, like anything else, is a process. Like anything else, you learn the process by using tried-and-true techniques from other successful salespeople, and you keep trying until you get better at it.

What follows is an example of growing my business when I used sales team members to help me achieve my goals and grow successfully. The challenge for me was hiring sales professionals who had the knowledge and experience to sell my team better than I could. I made a plan to prepare myself mentally for the changes. Once I was ready, I got the help of a trusted business mentor to help me source the right salespeople. I worked on developing my sales pitch for the ideal customer, and I provided this to the sales team to help them understand me and garner their ability to sell the business. I supplied each of them with a list of reasons to do business with me, and from there I worked with them on the objections I encountered the most. Finally, I provided details about the level of resources and expected revenue per resource with the goal to build a business that had greater than $1 million in revenue.

This approach was effective in getting myself and the team mentally prepared. Because I had equipped them with enough detail to understand what I wanted to achieve, they were able to move forward. I also had to prepare myself to perform a new role: hire salespeople who were better than me at selling and could expand the business beyond what I could ever do on my own. I also needed to make the necessary preparations to ensure I could fund this team of sales professionals. To do so, I had to take out a loan for the base salaries of the salespeople, along with the sales commissions that were funded by what they were able to help me achieve. After this experience, I advised others to the same: find the money to pay for a year of sales and then work the plan after mentally preparing for its implementation.

Chapter 16:

THE REALIZATION FRAMEWORK EXPERIENCE (RFE)

REALIZATION FRAMEWORK
E X P E R I E N C E®

The RFE was defined in the Introduction of this book. We are now going to take a deeper dive into the methodology's components. This concept grew directly from my earlier concept of The Art and Science of Vision to Reality!—which I use as my personal guide to get things done as envisioned. As the methodology became my personal foundation, I was able to turn it into an overall tool to facilitate entrepreneurs' efforts to achieve their dreams. I found I was successful moving entrepreneurs from one state to another—from their pain (no money, no time, and no support) to their prize (more money, more time, and more support) by taking their visualization to realization. As the time of writing this book, I trademarked The Art and Science of Vision to Reality! nearly eight years ago. It was the beginning of my stretch goal to help 1,000 small businesses a year meet their overall visions for their businesses.

Later, as I began to consider how to get entrepreneurs from their vision to living the reality of their dreams, I started by visualizing the steps I had taken in my own journey to realization. First, I **visualized** my desired future, then I **evaluated** who could help me get this future. I then **calculated** and forecast what I would need and how much I needed to get to the future, I **clarified** this future with a solid plan and then I **realized** my future with daily, weekly, and monthly actions. It worked for me and many others I helped before I even had clients. Therefore, I started applying those steps when I was working with clients to achieve their dreams.

With each of my business partners, I spend a great deal of time focusing on what they truly want—what they hope to accomplish not only in business but in life. The process takes time because though many entrepreneurs have numerous aspirations, they do not often have clarity on achieving those ends. They may allude to aspirations of comfort, happiness, financial stability, a life without worry, or a life full of success, even if they are not able to articulate those ideas or plan a way to get there.

Because not everyone is skilled in articulating their ideas, I find that some entrepreneurs have difficulty turning their objectives toward their desired reality. They have a frustrated vision because they understand it themselves but struggle to get others to understand it. That is where the RFE comes into play, offering clear guidance to achieve business ambitions and lifestyle dreams. The issue is, when entrepreneurs reach the point of being comfortable, free from worrying about bills, handling employees, and all the other aspects of business, they become uncomfortable! Being uncomfortable is good when growing, but not when all you are doing is churning with no evident growth and lost time. My goal is to help each entrepreneur visualize a happy, contented future and be comfortable there when it ultimately becomes their reality.

The Complications from Vision to Reality

Most entrepreneurs are highly skilled in a single area. That area of expertise is the one that likely inspired them to start their business in the first place. At first, they are excited to begin—ready to take on the world with dreams of success. Once they begin, reality soon sets in, and they have to face the fact that though they are highly skilled in one or two areas, they do not necessarily have all the skill sets to grow their business successfully.

Growing and developing the necessary skill sets involves investing in themselves to gain knowledge and learn how to become a proficient enough leader to achieve their dream. Another important aspect of being an adept leader is investing in people. Their people are not only their valued employees but are also those who influence them directly along with their target customers. Potential customers are especially tricky as they expect great experiences with every interaction, and successful entrepreneurs must learn to deliver those fulfilling customer experiences.

Often, making the crucial investments requires a complete behavioral shift in the entrepreneur to rise above the competition. Competition is tougher today than ever before in history. It comes from every direction—all day, every day. Gone are the days when the only competition came from local sources. Today's competition can come from anywhere around the globe, prompted and promoted by the ever-evolving stream of changing technology. Every entrepreneur must prepare to face the challenge of leveraging technology at every level. Problems arise when entrepreneurs use excuses like these:

- I am the only one who can get this done.
- I am the only one who can solve this problem.
- I am the only one who can handle this situation.

- I am the only one who can do this work.
- I am the only one with the expertise to resolve this issue.

Thinking they are the only one who can do things indicates a lack of trust in others who can truly help. When entrepreneurs make the necessary behavioral shifts and focus attention on their investment in their own team, they can get out of their own way. They learn to delegate the problem, situation, or work and allow others, who have the necessary knowledge and expertise, to come alongside them to make their job easier and their company more successful. The RFE teaches entrepreneurs to do just that: shift their behavior, releasing their fear of delegating, letting go, and getting the work done more effectively than they ever imagined (or thought they could accomplish on their own). It teaches them to trust!

When entrepreneurs employ the strategy behind the RFE methodology, they immediately gain the ability to overcome their existing internal struggles about their business and begin to focus on the job of running the business successfully. Doing so, with their needed behavior shifts, requires entrepreneurs to fight the urge to ignore the strategic steps they just learned, even when they don't appear to work instantaneously. They fight against the fear and follow through with the plan.

The process requires lowering expectations of perfection, not expecting 100-percent improvement after the first step and realizing momentum must be built throughout the journey. Progress has a long tail of incremental development before an upward trajectory of significant development that comes from the compound effect of positive actions focused on growing the business. The process means learning, truly learning, the skills needed. It means refusing to live in mere survival mode or take out loans (especially from family and friends) to maintain the status quo. It means learning how to understand financials (or any aspect of business with which they are unfamiliar), overcoming the issues, and making the necessary adjustments for success.

I mention financials specifically because this is often the greatest challenge and the principal area of concern. This is the area I am most approached to help someone solve. In fact, most of the time, a business owner is not my client, but they heard about my lending business. My lending business is tied to real estate, and when I tell them that I must have collateral and that we must do the loan through a personal guarantee, they don't want to go through that rigor. I also usually don't want to lend the money because they can't show me how much they really need with up-to-date financial documents. This is when they become a client—so I can help them with this process. When entrepreneurs fail to understand cash flow, accounts, receivables, payables, working capital, and other aspects of their financials, problems arise quickly, and panic often sets in for the long haul. The RFE methodology guides entrepreneurs to learn to understand their own finances, get out of the mess in which they find themselves, and develop a unique management system that works for their business and, in turn, produces an exceptional result.

Within the methodology, entrepreneurs learn to work *on* their business—not simply in it. As the company's founder, entrepreneurs must take on the role of the leader, not the role of an employee. Through the RFE, they achieve the maturity and expertise they need to succeed as an entrepreneur.

The overarching concept of the methodology is found in the two key components required for any business success: people and money. The people in the RFE are employees, mentors, customers, advisors or advisory boards, as well as anyone with whom the entrepreneur chooses to surround themself. The next step is to visualize a future with each of these people. Are they valuable to the realization of the dream? Or does it appear they will need to be replaced by others who can more effectively help achieve the dream?

The same concept applies to money and finances. After all, the way an entrepreneur's money flows through their business determines the health and growth of that business, similar to the effect of the people allowed to influence it. Both people and money are very visual components, which make them easy to see clearly as entrepreneurs face challenges, visualize the future, and take the necessary steps to succeed.

While those are the essentials of The Art and Science of Vision to Reality!, I knew there was much more as I developed my theory. On a flight to Miami, I pondered the question of the overall path from vision to reality. It was then that the steps to achieve the reality came to mind and became the realization framework, if you will. I added experience to the term because it is a journey from vision to reality. And the Realization Framework Experience was born.

As I mentioned earlier, the RFE methodology, in all its clarity, sprang from Desmond Tutu's famous quote: "There is only one way to eat an elephant: a bite at a time." Tutu's words remind everyone that though life is often challenging and filled with obstacles, any situation or circumstance can be overcome by moving forward one step at a time toward achieving the goal successfully. The RFE was developed with Tutu's "elephant" in mind, a way to guide entrepreneurs through the steps required to bring their vision to reality "one bite at a time." Below are the steps.

Steps of the Realization Framework Experience

1. <u>Visualize</u> the future with an aspirational set of goals.
2. <u>Evaluate</u> your people (owner, team, customers, advisors).
3. <u>Calculate</u> your cash flow.
4. <u>Clarify</u> the fog by developing a plan.
5. <u>Realize</u> the future by training to act daily, weekly, and monthly toward your company's aspirational goals.

These five simple steps are designed to guide entrepreneurs not only to a better business but to a superior life by allowing them to leverage my expertise in vision and strategy through this customizable framework. The RFE requires a full-on behavior shift that focuses entrepreneurs' attention on themselves and key people to gain the growth and achievement they desire. Through the RFE methodology, entrepreneurs take the necessary steps forward to accomplish their vision successfully.

The systems and strategies put in place with the RFE methodology allow entrepreneurs to continue to make money, but as an individual entrepreneur, you have to grind through them on your own. How do you do that? You create your own realization framework, which you then follow daily, weekly, and monthly.

Let's explore the steps in detail.

Step 1: Visualize

The first step requires you, as an entrepreneur, to visualize the future of your business with an aspirational set of goals. From day one, this means setting goals and establishing strategies for your business to achieve those goals. Remember, it is one step at a time—taken in the right direction.

Consider using SMART goals to help you plan and accomplish your goals: Specific (Significant), Measurable (Meaningful), Achievable (Attainable), Relevant (Realistic and Results-Based), and Time-Based (Targeted). For example, your goals for the interview process should include questions, answers, and tests for potential employees. However, before your goals are set, you should be able to create a picture in your mind's eye for what you aspire to be.

One of my client's, a general contractor, stated he wanted to be the largest minority-owned general contracting firm, mirroring Turner Construction, a multi-billion-dollar conglomerate that had been in business since the early 1900s. That is a big leap, and some would say it was too ambitious. But if small companies want to grow, they should develop a model that inspires them. The company was consistently maintaining over $1 million in annual revenue, but a clear vision allowed us to put a strategy in place for going from his current situation to a stabilization strategy and developing an overall growth plan with operations and people that would allow the organization to handle more business. Turner Construction had grown from a great deal of acquisitions and years of being in business. So, we developed a strategy for additional partners (joint ventures or acquiring other smaller companies) to meet the Turner dream in the next ten years. This is a great vision and can be achieved by applying the RFE methodology consistently.

Step 2: Evaluate

Evaluating your people—your team members, your customers and potential customers, your mentors, your advisors, and yourself as a leader—is an ongoing process for entrepreneurs. This not only includes current and potential customers but past customers as well. It is imperative to your success that you continually review customer feedback, both positive and negative. Doing so will help you determine issues and patterns. From there you can distinguish what is going well and focus on further developing those things, along with making positive changes about the things that are not going so well.

When selecting your advisors, choose carefully. In fact, I encourage business owners to set up a paid advisory board—one with members who are compensated well. Larger companies do this along with a board of directors to help guide the company to meet its goals.

Step 3: Calculate

To be successful, you always need to know where your money is coming from and where it is going. Remember, men lie, women lie, but numbers don't! This means you need to evaluate your current cash inflows and outflows continually. Evaluate your finances and operate by the numbers using your balance sheets, income statements, and cash flow statements for the current year as well as any past years. The most basic step is creating a budget!

Knowing your salaries, working capital, accounts receivable, accounts payable, EBITDA (earnings before interest, taxes, depreciation, and amortization), order to cash timing, costs of goods sold, and more is the key to validating your current measurements against industry best-in-class. With this data, you can move your company forward with greater success. Also, I see too many clients with accounts receivables that are way too high as they scramble to pay bills, especially payroll.

Step 4: Clarify

I use the term "clear the fog" because the concept of fog is easily understood. Everyone has experienced fog, as well as the clear view after the fog burns off, which makes it an exceptional visual. In the fog, you can see very little ahead of you, by your sides, or behind you. You cannot see your destination, even if you are close to it. When you can clear the fog, your circumstances change; the sun comes out and you can see where you are going clearly as the sun shines on the path to your success.

Often in business, clearing the fog comes from a dialogue with a trusted advisor or colleague. In the midst of the conversation, the fog clears, and you can once again see where you need to go to move forward. You can once again visualize the future, take the next steps, and go realize the future you have dreamed of. Clearing the fog has the potential to take you from vision to reality in both business and life.

So, how do you do it? Begin with a plan, then organize your company to eliminate employee, customer, and cash flow problems. Your new plan should include hiring, firing, and upskilling your employees; reorganizing your employees based on their strengths and gaps that need to be filled; acquiring external expert support (e.g., mentor, accountant, lawyer, sales manager, marketing manager, investors); and developing a capital plan.

The result should be a clearly understood set of goals and actions for which each "actor" (the employees, advisors, etc.) knows their role and is held accountable for fulfilling their agreed-upon duties (the steps to "eating the elephant" on your way to the dream state for your business).

Step 5: Realize

Realizing the future requires training both the entrepreneur and their employees to act daily, weekly, and monthly toward the company's aspirational goals. This is the step where your vision starts to take shape as your reality—in other words, your happy ending.

In this step, I work with entrepreneurs, like you, guiding what is essentially the kickoff of your new and improved company as the aspirational goals, actions, accountability, and responsibilities come together for everyone in the company. Here, to continue to grow successfully, entrepreneurs need to focus on people—employees and customers—and, in turn, become better business owners as a result of the RFE.

The Result of The Realization Framework Experience

The results of The RFE include more time, more money, and more support so entrepreneurs can stop working and start living! Through The Realization Framework Experience, business owners realize their dream lifestyle by eliminating daily stresses concerning cash, employees, and customers. They define their vision of an achievable future and begin the journey toward the realization of that future. Essentially, through the five simple steps of the RFE, entrepreneurs move from an unclear present to a crystal-clear future as they work and learn through the steps.

Business can be one of the most powerful forces for good, and with the RFE, you can grow your business and transform the lives of your customers, your employees, and yourself. Take the Visionnaire Scorecard at https://visionnaire.scoreapp.com/ to see how well you score in each of the RFE areas.

PART 3:

How to Prevent Backsliding

I am a Visionnaire—and so are you if you choose to follow the principles of the RFE. What makes me or you a Visionnaire? I am a Visionnaire because I was able to get more money, more time, and more support to create prosperity beyond my visions.

The word "Visionnaire" stems from the visioning of the RFE and creates the status of someone who has made it financially and has become a key influencer in their industry or market. I became a Visionnaire by leveraging all my visioning exercises from 2008 to now. When I began visioning, my vision was to change the world one person at a time. Today, my vision has evolved to change *my* world one person at a time through meaningful, impactful, and engaging relationships and moments.

For example, one of my first visions was to grow my salary by $25,000 per year. Though it sounds linear, when I tracked it, it was not; it was rather an upward curve that has exceeded what I envisioned, not only in salary but in career accomplishments as well. It took several years to gain the trajectory needed, and I often felt like I would never achieve the goal. There were many times when I stopped measuring because my visioning was not going as planned and challenged my self-esteem. I stopped focusing on the goal in a literal sense and kept focus on the path (vision) of my overall goal to be a leader in my industry and a key influencer in the project management profession. I stuck to my principles of organizing my path with the people and cash flow needed to meet the goal. Then I received a promotion to Vice President, Project Management Office. I had almost forgotten about the goal of $25,000 per year—but I didn't lose the habits I put in place to get there. One day, as I do often, I looked at the notebook where I keep my goals to see what I had achieved from the time I made the goal. I then mapped my income for each year after I made that goal and was pleasantly surprised to see that I had exceeded my goal. It took the four years of my income growth taking a northward trajectory, but that was what I needed to meet the goal since the previous years were somewhat flat and sporadic. I followed my principles of the RFE methodology, stuck with it, and never gave up, finally exceeding my goal. You can do the same if you also follow the principles of The RFE methodology and do not backslide.

The Process of Preventing Backsliding

Preventing backsliding is a three-pronged approach. And it begins with you.

Step 1

The first step to preventing backsliding is developing habits. You must always be at work on yourself to become a better leader. As you are working through the methodology, especially the first time, you need to take the time to think about the impact you are making on the organization, as well as what you are learning. It is critical that you learn how to best use your time, tools, and talent based on your strengths. If your strength is business development, you should be focused on that aspect of the business, not running around doing other tasks you could have organized and delegated for others in your organization to accomplish. Look in the mirror and ask, "Am I being the best leader I can be?" You should be able to measure progress over time, looking at your earnings, your employees, and your organization. Is the company getting better? Are circumstances and processes improving?

Step 2

The second area is looking at measures, asking yourself, "Am I using the right processes to help myself and my company?" One of the benefits of the RFE is daily activities that allow you to sit down and determine what you are going to accomplish on a day-to-day basis.

Next is the monthly milestone chart. You need to do both the daily activities and the monthly milestone chart. When you do, you are behaving like a larger business, and you can definitely adjust when needed. Put yourself in the leadership role, focusing on your unique ownership responsibilities. Have your company leaders focus on their distinct responsibilities. Leverage the knowledge of your board of advisors regarding quarterly responsibilities so that you build in accountability while maintaining your defined role and completing the tasks you need to fulfill.

Step 3

Finally, the third step to prevent backsliding and stay on track is creating accountability with something like the CEO Dashboard. The dashboard contains a series of measurements that allow you to stay on track and provide a visual of your business. This tool is an effective Excel spreadsheet, and I work with my business partners to customize their spreadsheets based on the measures they want to achieve. They use the dashboard to have a near real-time understanding of where they are doing well and where they are falling short.

***

I encourage every leader to run through the set measures of their RFE methodology for a minimum of a year before making any major adjustments or stopping. It is important to stay with the measurements you set in the onset of the process. You might want to make an adjustment to a measurement because it seems too difficult to reach. To you, it might seem like it will always look red, but I say live with it for now, because you are still in a learning process the first time you go through the RFE. If you change it early on and make it easier to reach, you are not growing your business, you are not helping yourself, and you are not being the leader you can be. It is okay to have difficult targets in the beginning while you discern what you can and cannot achieve.

Chapter 17:

FACE THE MIRROR!

ook in the mirror and tell yourself: YOU are a Visionnaire. Get used to doing it!

Most entrepreneurs work in the business and not on the business. They act as technicians while trying to be entrepreneurs. My goal is to get you, the Visionnaire, to face the mirror and move from being a technician to the entrepreneur, a mature business owner who takes action.

It all goes back the question of what you, the entrepreneur, hope to achieve with your business. Many, maybe even you, will say "I want a $12-million business" because you want the lifestyle you believe comes with those earnings. The truth is, you must decide if you really want to work to achieve that end or if you are simply hoping to sound like an entrepreneur and play at the role with that goal. If you really want to grow, you need to face the mirror and accept that it will take time to accomplish your goals.

You have to see yourself differently. When you face the mirror, do not think of yourself as a business owner or entrepreneur; you are a Visionnaire. Once you identify with being a Visionnaire, you need to identify the habits of the Visionnaire and match your actions to that Visionnaire mindset.

The Habits and Mindset of a Visionnaire

A Visionnaire exhibits the following habits and characteristics:

- You are well-organized.
- You are persistent in your pursuits.
- You have good habits taking care of first things first.
- You develop innovative ways to operate your business.
- You are willing to take risks.
- You run your company with enthusiasm.
- You are focused.
- You have a good plan.
- You inspire others and they follow or emulate you.
- You are willing to listen to and learn from others.
- Others want to learn from you.

From that list, a willingness to listen to others and learn from them is key. You may believe you have it all, but if you are not in the space you want to be in terms of growing your business, you have to face the mirror. What do you need to do to become a Visionnaire and take your company to the next level?

This is where the feedback from your employees, the feedback from your peer group and network, and the feedback you get from your advisors become key components of facing yourself in the mirror and identifying your blind spots. Everyone has unique blind spots. As I was building my business, my personal blind spot was that I did not like conflict; therefore, I tried to avoid conflict as much as possible. An advisor helped me develop some conflict resolution techniques, and then I was able deal with conflict. Now, I welcome conflict because conflict is the convergence of the passion between two entities trying to achieve the same goals.

One time when I experienced conflict with a client, I was managing a large project at a well-known food processing and distribution company.

There was a major conflict in which the leader of the supply chain project made assumptions about the plans I had for the organization. My boss was also involved, calling me worried about the assertions this individual had made to his boss (who was a shared boss of the supply chain leader and my boss). I reassured my boss, "Listen, I have learned how to deal with conflicts using these techniques. Let me share with you what I plan to do. Once it is done, let's talk again."

I went to the leader of the supply chain project who had made the assumptions. Using a conflict resolution model that I had learned, I asked him to explain the problem as he understood it, tell me the facts as he knew them, explain how he felt, and share what he wanted. After he spoke and I listened, I stated the problem as I understood it, the facts I knew, how I felt, and what I wanted. After the conversation, the whole conflict was deemed a total misunderstanding.

Afterward, my boss, who was nearly in tears, offered, "I don't know how you do what you do."

It was important for me to learn conflict resolution because you cannot grow personally or professionally if you do not deal with conflict well. I had to face the mirror with the feedback given to me to understand what I was good at and what areas needed improvement. I learned you can face conflict with a degree of courage if you have the right tools in place.

One final point I'd like to add about facing the mirror comes from a quote by Jim Rohn: "If you really want to do something, you will find a way; if you don't, you'll find an excuse." When you see yourself as a Visionnaire, you will no longer look for excuses but will continuously look to build vision upon vision upon vision—and lead others to do the same.

Chapter 18:

▶ TRUST THE PROCESS ▶

ntrepreneurs must trust the process over time—at least giving it one year—performing the process daily. This means you must follow the RFE and work with me for at least a year before you get the ultimate results you envisioned. This gives you time to develop habits, validate the measures, and ensure a level of accountability. The goal is to play out the entire framework and make the new habits routine for the owner as well as the leaders of the company. It's the habits that will take you far. I once read, and now wholeheartedly believe, that people do not decide their futures; they decide their habits, and their habits decide their futures. There is a direct link between your vision and your habits. That's why we work together for accountability when it comes to the habits until they are a part of you.

The initial agreement involves the company owner meeting with me so that I can understand exactly what they want and how they see their company growing in the next three to five years. I want to know not only what they hope for their business in the future but also **why** they see the company that way, what they have tried in the past (whether it worked or did not work), and what role they see themselves playing in the future of the company. I also attempt to bring to the surface any fears, doubts, or apprehensions they may have about themselves, the company, the market they serve, or their employees.

From these conversations, I begin developing the vision of the company in words with the owner. This is an iterative process until we have a solid agreement on the articulation of the vision. My goal then is to present that information so that the owner understands that although I may have put the materials together describing what the vision is, the vision is entirely their own.

I had one client tell me the RFE is simply a numbers game, a predictable trajectory for how you get into business. Then he started touting word of mouth as the best way to gain new business.

So, I asked, "How is word of mouth different than paying a salesperson? A salesperson can work and get more reach and still work the sales that come from word of mouth."

The client then responded, "Well, this is a blue-collar business, a different type of business. This is my experience, and this is how it works."

I replied, "Yes, this is *how it works for mediocrity. Your sales have plateaued for the last three years.* Are you afraid to try something different because when you tried something different and it didn't work, you felt like you'd exhausted all possibilities? You have got to trust this process and learn from it, not just jump away! When you start most things, if they work really well, you get a hockey stick effect: the sharp rise after a flat period. The problem is, most people give up before they see the growth!"

Getting Past the Objections

To overcome a client's objections, I typically ask if I can provide a step-by-step process (the RFE methodology) to grow their business in which they will allow me to take the lead on people and finances and serve as chairman of the advisory board for one year.

The answer is usually "yes," primarily because I commit to working before I discuss any compensation and only look at developing a contract for the advisory services once we start working. I then ask for all the financial information available from the last few years and a list of all the key employees in the company who I can access for their perspectives and the details I need to begin a forensic review of the current operation.

At first, there may be resistance if the owner believes that reviewing the current operation does not show how the business can grow. They think they can just get more jobs and that's the only piece of the puzzle to grow. And that would grow the business at the top level, but is the business profitable already? How do you know? Where are you leaking money? One of the areas I discuss is accounts receivable. I look at everything and follow the process I encouraged.

For one client who held several hundred thousand dollars in accounts receivable, here are the steps I took in the process.

1. After getting the financials from their QuickBooks system, I set the numbers aside. My next step was to set up a series of interviews with each of the business's key leaders and office personnel. I asked simple questions about how they did their jobs, what their understanding of the company's goals were (most had no idea!), what they wanted as an employee, and what their feelings were about the company and the company leadership. I also asked what they liked, what they didn't like, and, most importantly, how they would improve the company with their contributions if they had the skills or authority in the decision-making. Employees who are on the frontline with customers can give you information about what is going on that you can't ascertain any other way.

2. Next, I went back to the numbers and asked if their accountants or bookkeepers could provide balance sheets, income statements, details on accounts receivables, and details of their overall debt picture. Here, I looked at the days outstanding for invoices, as

well as categories of debt for short-term and long-term. I looked for seasonal income patterns and asked questions about customers: Was there a customer or set of customers who contributed a significant portion of the yearly revenue? Were there customers who cost the company money?

3. Once I had those answers, I performed a Pareto analysis (based on the idea that 80 percent of the customers make up 20 percent of the revenue and 20 percent of the customers make up 80 percent of the revenue). From this customer analysis, I helped them determine who must be treated with white gloves to maintain a positive relationship (the 20 percent of customers who make up 80 percent of the revenue), who needed to have their prices raised (the customers benefitting from the same delivery costs as those customers who represented 80 percent of revenue), and who no longer needed to be serviced (customers who only represent 20 percent of the products *and* cost more to serve than they bring the company in revenue). This analysis can be done by any entrepreneur who wants to evaluate the types of customers they want to develop marketing and growth plans with (customers who fit the profile of the major portion of revenue). The key here is to root out the costly customers and learn about their profile to put measures in place to avoid them. This will help mitigate issues with a large accounts receivables number by avoiding the specific demographic of people less likely to pay.

4. After I explore my findings, I develop a report and recommend a plan of action: the RFE, steps one through four. This is when I put my findings into play. I work directly with the head of the company to inform and stay in communication with the team. What follows is an example of the first meeting. The other meetings follow the same pattern, and we adjust as necessary.

We begin with an announcement about why I am there to help them and what we hope to achieve. Next, we explain that I will be leading a weekly meeting to discuss several topics:

1. Company Announcements
2. Customer Concerns (complaints with remediation plans, lessons learned, and success stories)
3. Employee Concerns (company updates, expectations, recognition, policies, etc.)
4. Actions from the previous meetings
5. New Business (sales wins/losses, opportunities, performance toward goals)
6. Roundtable (to get everyone's participation) Action Items and Next Steps
7. A Rallying Cry to close the meeting: Never Settle!

It is my belief that you must have a rallying cry and a set of values everyone in the company can get behind.

Once the weekly meeting is established, I also work with the leaders to develop a daily routine, as well as monthly and quarterly routines. It can be daunting at first. Why all these meetings? One of my favorite quotes that I often use with my business partners comes from the movie *Behind Enemy Lines*, starring Gene Hackman, who was having a heated exchange with a young lieutenant, Burnett, on the importance of routine. Burnett was burned out from boredom because he had to keep doing the same boring activities every day and could not understand how the routine was necessary to help them win a war. Burnett wanted action! Gene Hackman's response was, "It's the routine that keeps us alive. We ARE at war!" I love this quote because we are at war trying our best to win the game of business against competition!

Many books and business quotes reference the similarities of war. Getting my business partners to see we are at war is my job. If they aren't meeting their goals, they are losing the war. I push and push the routine because I have seen companies that are doing well but are not prepared when issues arise regarding collecting money. They weren't streamlined to weather the storm. Their routine is the foundation. Once we have a strong foundation, we can grow from there. I work with my business partners to build a full calendar with daily, weekly, monthly, and quarterly activities with roles and responsibilities for each. This approach sets expectations and helps companies behave like larger corporations. Believe it or not, building a full calendar of focused activities actually gives you more time for yourself and other things you want to spend time doing. You can easily get there by trusting the process and giving it enough time to work.

Chapter 19:

DO IT ANYWAY!

I f the methodology doesn't feel right because it's new, do it anyway! Your emotions can easily stop your growth. Often entrepreneurs are discouraged because something doesn't feel right when it's new. If you feel that way, don't stop the process; do it anyway! You can't expect everything to work immediately. And when it doesn't, you may think it doesn't feel right. In most cases, those feelings are because what you are trying is new. You haven't tried it before, and you are ready to give up because it didn't work in the first month. Honestly, in most cases, it's not going to work in the first month. In fact, most business relationships take two years to cultivate—going from introduction to contract takes, on average, two years.

Confirmation bias and status quo bias are the two cognitive dissonance behaviors that most often keep entrepreneurs from moving forward. These must be acknowledged and managed to continue your path and avoid backsliding.

Avoiding the Manifestation of Change

Often in my conversations with my mentees—those who work directly for me or individuals who are struggling with changing the way they do things—I say, "Hey, you know that feeling you have right now in the pit of your stomach? That is growth." They want a better way of doing things, but they are familiar with the way they have always done things, and that makes it difficult to change.

I once had an employee who told me she almost hit the floor when I told her she was going to represent me at a meeting. I explained that what she felt was growth hitting her, an experience that is unfamiliar to most people. I knew this employee was ready, but she didn't. I would never risk my reputation by letting someone represent me who could do harm to both of us.

One way to continue to grow is to get comfortable with being uncomfortable. There is nothing more uncomfortable than change. Think about it. If you start an exercise regimen and eat right, you challenge your body. Why? You want to have better muscle tone, enhance your health, and strengthen your heart, so to accomplish the goal, you have to put the heart and the muscles through their paces. You must provide resistance against what your body is used to; you have to break down those muscles to build them up. It is the same with your mind—with what you are trying to attack, with what you are trying to achieve. You must break down the old habits before you can break through the changes to new and improved practices.

When you choose to work with me through the RFE, much of what I teach will not be comfortable for you, but to accomplish your goals, you have to just do it anyway. You will eventually find yourself on the other side of it, after doing the uncomfortable things daily, weekly, monthly, and quarterly, marveling at how much you have achieved. After all, the first step in any journey, no matter how long, is simply the first step. Just do it anyway!

You may have to fight your desire to keep the status quo or continue the way you were doing it. It is not unusual. Humans are creatures of habit, wired to use the least amount of energy to get what we need. Do not fall for it. You have to be different. You have to change, especially if you want those who are following you to change. You must get in the habit of doing it anyway! Earlier, we discussed the habits and characteristics of a Visionnaire—innovative, inspiring, persistent, organized, enthused, focused, and open to listening to others—and you have to embrace those characteristics, keep at it, and face the changes head-on to do it anyway.

Planning is so important in this process of facing change and doing it anyway. Let me share just how important. I take these key lessons from own experiences managing mergers and acquisitions. These lessons come from my analysis after the fact and show the outcomes from four different types of acquisitions over a two-year period.

Case One

In this case, the acquisition was internal to the United States. I discovered a key lesson in large cost: $135,000 that was not counted in the costs of the project. The overall overhead for the project management leadership, which includes planning and organizing resources toward the desired goals, was around 30 percent, right at industry standards for projects of a certain size. The overall costs after planning and executing this project were ideal with a 0.24 percent margin.

Case Two

The next case was a Finland and Russia project. We proceeded through the planning phases but learned lessons because we underestimated the time required to mentor less experienced people. Our goal was to use less costly resources in the locations, while simultaneously growing the competency for certain projects. We assumed, as it was an independent project, that there would be no other impacts, but there was a dual environment conflict regarding an upgrade to the project that resulted in lots of meetings about coordinating disparate geographic resources and communications. In the end, the budget went slightly over by 21 percent. I like to manage costs between plus or minus 15 percent with a complex project. However, the project management remained consistently near 30 percent.

Case Three

The third case did very well at 7 percent of the budget. Many of the functions were to be handled by one set of resources but were handled by local resources in Korea, which helped a great deal in keeping us under budget for this project.

Case Four

The last case was in Norway and went more than 50 percent over budget with a 43 percent overhead in project leadership. Why? The business got used to us delivering but thought the costs were high. They wondered why they should pay for 30 percent overhead for planning and wanted to squeeze this to keep costs down. The lack of planning was revealed in issues with some local laws that would have been easily understood had we done the proper planning. This was our first time in this region, so we could not make the same assumptions. Because we didn't take the time to develop a good plan, the project timeline extended by 40 percent and the overall budget was exceeded by more than 50 percent.

The lesson learned here was that planning is at the foundation of success in anything you do. You cannot skip it! It is the basis of the RFE when you find that clearing the fog is purely a planning exercise that comes after you understand your cash flow and people needs. It's tying those things into the overall vision. Planning is essential for leveraging or best using your time, as well as all your resources' time. With the proper planning, everyone knows what they are doing and what they hope to achieve. You may not tell everyone down to the last detail, but they know exactly what their daily tasks are, as well as their weekly and monthly tasks. They know what they are seeking to achieve because you, as the leader, have told them, worked with them, and helped them understand their role in achieving the overall vision for the organization.

A planning mindset also allows you to perform better. It is true for athletes who plan, exercise, and eat to achieve optimal performance, and it is true for your business. You need to feed it the right ingredients, nurture it, and care for it the right way under the best conditions. In doing so, you work your plan toward success.

When you perform the exercises of the RFE—daily, weekly, monthly, and quarterly—you learn new habits, change from old ways of working, and develop planning methods to avoid cognitive dissonance behaviors like confirmation bias and status quo bias. When you do it anyway, pushing through the changes and breaking down the challenges, you step into new and better habits that will allow you and your business to grow and succeed.

Chapter 20:

▶ RECOGNIZE GROWTH ▶

As previously stated, if you feel uneasy in your gut, it is probably an indicator of growth! If you make changes and have success in the first month, keep going. If you make changes and don't have success in the first month, keep going. Trust the process and do it anyway. Get out of your head and don't let your fear or lack of patience take control. Trust that the process is working. Talk to other successful entrepreneurs and businesspeople as much as you can. They can encourage you to keep moving forward—with patience and without fear. They can help you understand timing and recognize growth.

Use your measures as a guide. Let them judge your progress and remove the self-judgement. When I golf, the course or range finder will show the distance from where I am to the pin. In several cases, my visual judgement said the information from the range finder was incorrect. It might read 150 yards and I think it doesn't feel like 150 yards because 150 yards usually seems farther or shorter. Then I would select a club other than my seven iron (my 150-yard club). After I hit the ball, the result is always somewhat predictable. I was either longer or shorter because I allowed myself to use my own judgement instead of letting the data from several sources tell me exactly what I needed. One of the reasons this happens is because I don't golf enough, but if I want to improve my game, I must play more, learn my distances, and trust the data. Business owners must do the same. Get out of your head and trust the measures.

At a minimum, there are four major groups of measurement every business should have at their disposal. These measurements follow the RFE and include evaluating your people and calculating your cash flow. The major categories for measurement are:

1. Financial Measures
2. Employee Measures
3. Customer Measures
4. Sales Measures

I spend time developing the specific measures with my business partners that they need to focus on. Each business is unique, so the measures really depend on the company and the goals of the company when it comes to specific metrics in these areas. However, there are some baseline measurements companies must have in each category.

For financial measures, leaders should ensure their business has positive cash flow. This is a basic measure to see whether you have more money coming in than going out. Other measures can show how profitable the company is. The leader must showcase metrics focused on the company's profitability and ability to pay back debt should the company need to seek additional funding.

Another measure in the calculating cash flow area of the RFE are the sales measures. Sales are the heart of the company. I was once told that we all work for the salespeople in the organization—without them, there is no us. Each must be measured, and, in these cases, I will focus on the sales measures and discuss customer measures as they relate to knowing the company's sales personnel and existing customers. Sales measures should be at the top of your financial goals. Most people state the size of their company based on its annual revenue. It is crucial to know whether the business is on track for the company goals.

For example, a company with a $1-million goal must have sales quotas broken into measures for daily sales, weekly sales, monthly sales, and quarterly sales. You can detect early whether the company is on track for sales by measuring within these units. Most sales cycles don't allow leaders to predict sales at such a granular level, but over time, they can adjust their measurements and targets based on how they performed previously. The knowledge gained and the relationships developed can then help with planning.

When I discuss the areas of measures with business partners that have to do with knowing their people, I tell them that employees and customers are the best measures for growth. Why? Well, for instance, you probably can't effectively measure your success based on your advisory board relationships unless each advisor has specific goals, but to get to the heart of your cash flow and operation ecosystem, employees and customers are the groups that matter the most.

For employee measures, you want to know how much you are spending per employee and determine if your sales per employee is consistent with the average in your industry. Employee attrition or retention measures can also help you determine whether you have a good track record for keeping employees. If you are constantly working on turnover for employees, something is wrong within your hiring practices and judgement. Perhaps you aren't paying enough for the job or not giving enough attention to the employee. There must be measures for employee turnover and how new employees are adapting to your company's culture. Are they constantly late? Do you allow this to happen? There are many fundamental measurements that can help you see and understand how you are handling your employees.

Customer measures are crucial as well. You could even argue that these are actual measures of your quality and delivery capabilities. Complaints and returns should be measured too, as you can easily lose sight of the fact that the people who complain are the ones who are actually doing you a favor. When customers complain, they are giving you specific details about areas in which you can improve. When you resolve those issues, you may have saved that relationship along with ten other relationships you didn't even know about. On the flip side, there are those who may not complain but will simply leave and never do business with you again. Each customer, the ones who complain and the ones who don't, impacts hundreds and thousands of others by providing good or bad feedback, whether to you, friends, family, or colleagues. Customer measures, including complaints and returns, must receive heavy focus if your business is to succeed.

Focus on your measures rather than allowing your gut feeling to throw you off course. The measures provide an accurate picture of what is going on in your business and will help you recognize growth as it happens.

Chapter 21:

THE FIRST MILLION IS THE HARDEST

E ntrepreneurs should understand that earning the first million is always the hardest. It is the magical measure of success: $1 million. It is what every entrepreneur in their business beginnings wants to achieve.

I've heard this from others before, and I've also experienced it. Even though $1 million is not what it used to be, everyone wants to be a millionaire. The problem is that you can't become a millionaire and be comfortable. You'll have to keep grinding.

When entrepreneurs talk about their businesses, they say that once you've made your first million, it'll get easier. Why? Because the systems and team members they put in place have allowed them to grow and make money. And they also learned as they worked through those systems. That's how they made it to the first million.

How do you do that? You create your overall realization framework, and you follow it on a daily, weekly, and monthly basis. Everyone who reports to you, everyone who works for you, everyone who is advising you, and everyone in your inner circle must know what your realization framework vision looks like. They need to be speaking the same truth as you and moving toward your goals at all times.

Your first step is to review your vision and articulate it clearly for yourself. It should be a compelling vision that, once achieved, will give you a business worth millions of dollars. If your vision is to thrive in a way similar to a successful, existing company, and the company you aspire to is worth millions or billions, then you don't have to assign a number to your goal. You should assume that if you perform like the billion-dollar company and lead like the billion-dollar company owner, you will automatically be positioned to make millions of dollars in similar fashion.

Once you can clarify your vision, including what your company and your life will look like in five years, you can begin to work on articulating this vision to everyone involved. I work with my business partners extensively until they see on paper what is possible. For example, showing them an increasing income chart year over year using their last two years of income (where their top line is annual revenue), then projecting the next three to five years with growth until they can see the point when they could reach or far surpass their million-dollar mark. An example chart looks like this:

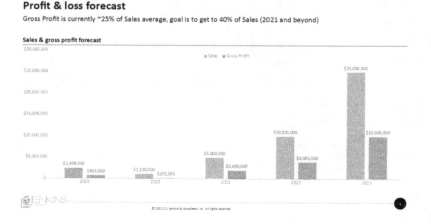

Profit & loss forecast

Gross Profit is currently ~25% of Sales average, goal is to get to 40% of Sales (2021 and beyond)

Sales & gross profit forecast

As you can see, this chart shows the leap from $1.5 million to $5 million, then $10 million, then $25 million in annual revenue. This simple chart is the beginning of achieving the vision and setting the stage for others who are ready and poised to follow you. Who wouldn't want to be a part of something this great?

Once you can see the vision clearly yourself, your next move is to develop a compelling story to tell your current team. You should also be ready to tell the story to others who are necessary in the process of accomplishing the vision: future employees, investors, and even family members. Remember, everyone loves a winner, and the prospect of achieving greatness will help everyone get on board quickly. In addition to the chart above, we add elements to show how we get that growth.

- Break down the $5 million per year into smaller time and dollar increments:
  - Months = $417,000
  - Weeks = $96,000
  - Days = $14,000
- Business Development is required full-time. It may require more than one person, so you should consider a sales professional long-term.
- Each week, the CEO develops a list of potential clients who add up to $96,000 or more in various lines of business. Take this example of a general contracting business with three lines of business:
  - Commercial = $72,000 – An achievable goal with very large jobs.
  - Residential = $24,000 – Rehabs and new construction projects are the targets here.
  - Maintenance = $5,000 – Many small jobs available at this level working with landlords and property owners.

- Beginning, for example, with this process in January 2021 (keep in mind all planned personnel are not place), you can expect an upward trajectory to begin in the second quarter of 2022.
- In the second half of 2022, begin looking for partners or acquisition targets to fit into the overall strategy. An example would be a well-functioning firm with a history of steady business, little to no debt, and a specialty in either commercial or residential projects with annual revenues at or above our targets.

Here you begin to see why the first million is the hardest. In this case, the company actually achieved their first million but was consistently hovering right above $1 million. It had all the same problems of trying to grow but with more difficulty. They wanted to get to the next level of $5 million, which was their new first million. The most difficult task to achieve in this example is getting the business leader to set their primary focus on creating $96,000 of business each week, a considerable increase from the existing level of $29,000 of business each week (average derived from $1.5 million annually divided by the fifty-two weeks of the year). The company is already accustomed to generating the lower level of income, and in many cases can produce a little more, but now they are faced with filling a gap of $67,000 per week to achieve the next step in their vision.

The prospect is equally frightening and compelling, but it also makes the vision real and tangible, laying out a goal that must be accomplished to bring the vision to fruition. Each week, I worked with this entrepreneur to stretch him, to show him how he would fill these gaps. He had to look at different avenues like increasing his focus on more commercial business and less residential business. He had to learn to say "no" to some smaller residential projects while saying "yes" to full house rehabilitations that paid more in shorter amounts of time.

When we showed this to his team, it was frightening for them as well, but after reviewing the organizational chart and showing them how they could grow into positions of leadership, as well as glean other benefits from the growth of the organization, they were excited to do their part. Having these details in hand also excites potential partners and advisors who want to be part of a winning team with a winning strategy.

After the Fact: A Testimonial from Calvin Snowden, CEO of BDFS

BDFS Group is a team of construction professionals that was founded in 2008 and is based in Philadelphia, Pennsylvania. BDFS provides clients with top-quality services in residential and commercial projects of various sizes throughout the Greater Philadelphia area.

Calvin Snowden, CEO of BDFS Group, explains the company was "looking to expand the business." The truth was, BDFS was "growing fast but needed capital and talent to keep up with demand."

BDFS had the good problem of an explosion in business with back-loaded contracts (to be paid when the jobs were completed), but they did not have enough people to see the work through nor enough capital for supplies.

Jenkins & Associates helped create a partnership and line of credit to fund these projects while the CEO focused on acquiring more business and more talent.

As a result, BDFS is now thriving with the ability to complete all the jobs. In addition, they now have a model that is flexible and ready for additional growth.

Snowden says, "The capital Jenkins & Associates helped us obtain was crucial to the success of our business. I am glad we consulted with Curtis Jenkins, and we will continue to leverage his experience to help us grow our business."

Chapter 22:

VISION TO ROADMAP

To keep from backsliding, entrepreneurs need to keep their vision clear and the roadmap free of obstructions. Entrepreneurs often backslide because they have difficulty keeping their vision clear. As a result, their roadmap to success becomes littered with obstacles that prevent them from arriving at their destination. It is imperative that entrepreneurs map out a clear vision of what they want their reality to be. Once the map is complete, the vision should be revisited daily, weekly, and monthly, and the map should be adjusted based on the available metrics.

On my own journey, the vision evolved over time, and the map was adjusted to keep me moving forward on the road to success. Earlier I shared how I got started on my business vision. However, here I share my personal vision as it relates to my career in corporate America.

My personal Visionnaire story begins in 2002, nearly twenty years ago. I had just lost my job. I developed a plan to get employment, and I was able to do so quickly following my daily routine of writing down names of people who could help me, calling them in the morning to share my story and see if they could help me find a job, trolling the internet for jobs, sending in applications, and getting up every day to go speak to people directly in person about hiring me. It was all uncomfortable at first, but I did it, and the fruit came two months after I lost my job. I wanted to grow in my field of project management, so I created a vision that included being a vice president of the project management office at a global company headquartered in the Northeast, Mid-Atlantic, or Southeast part of the United States. The company had to support my values as I was volunteering to help make the world and myself better through my leadership in Black Data Processing Associates. In addition to achieving this vision, I wanted to increase my salary by $25,000 per year along the journey in total compensation. I mapped out the journey each year with a table that provided a roadmap for how I wanted to progress in salary, bonus, perks, and position. After my apartment caught fire earlier that same year, I sold my rental property and did not account for the capital gains tax that would later haunt me. I received a letter from the IRS and read it to believe that they were going to garnish my wages for $425 per paycheck. What I missed was that they took everything except for $425—which was now my biweekly paycheck! I needed a plan, and I needed one fast!

To be successful, I needed to organize myself and develop a clear plan to achieve my vision. Here are the stops I took:

1. Research project management careers paying $175,000 and above
2. Determine gaps between my current skills and experience and the careers researched
3. Fill gaps through:
    a. Internal responsibility changes
    b. Education (low or no cost) – YouTube is an awesome resource
    c. Classroom training – key courses that add value to my experience
    d. On-the-job – training courses
    e. Networking – people who can help me get where I want to go

I looked at the people who could help me, but first I developed a list of prospective companies I could work for. They were sponsoring companies for my volunteer organization, and since I was responsible for the organization's strategy as Vice President of Strategy and four-time winner of Chapter of the Year when I was President of the Philadelphia chapter, I was not invisible to those organizations. These prospects ran the gamut of hot to cold. The hot prospects were companies that had previously expressed an interest in me during our annual career fairs and also had a key person of influence I had a direct relationship with. Below is my list of prospects.

Current Prospects:

1. J.P. Morgan Chase (Hot)
2. Cigna (Hot)
3. Wyeth (Warm)
4. Wachovia (Warm)
5. Johnson & Johnson (Warm)
6. Monsanto (Cold)
7. American Express (Cold)
8. Dell (Cold)
9. Rohm and Haas (Warm)
10. Allstate (Warm)

With this goal, I got the job with Fleet Credit Card, a major sponsor for my volunteer organization, BDPA. I got the job with a reference from a former colleague. I never changed my goals, and I ended up at Rohm and Haas for a few years until an acquisition by Dow Chemical gave me an incentive to leave and immediately create Jenkins & Associates, Inc and secure my first client (Amtrak). This is when I began sourcing project managers. Strategy and business advisement services came later in 2010. I worked for another two companies after Amtrak, and I ended up exceeding my goal of increasing my income by $25,000 per year, but it was not a linear process. I did not reach the level of Vice President nor the mathematical equivalent of $25,000 per year until 2020 (a figure that combined my business income and my position as a Vice President of Project Management), although my first target date was 2016.

The lesson here is that, like life, your plans are not linear. I went years without more than 2–3 percent in growth but made up for it in the later years, just like the hockey stick reference that I made earlier. While going through this process, I also had a tremendous amount of debt from all the mistakes I made with finances. So, I managed my cash flow with the snowball method of removing debt made popular by Dave Ramsey.

I also made sure that I surrounded myself with people who were also aspirational and could hold me accountable for my goals. Everything that I am sharing in this book about becoming a Visionnaire I did to achieve personal and professional success myself. I created a roadmap and worked the plans, measuring each month and year. My strategy didn't always go as planned. I made some tremendous personal sacrifices and my own share of mistakes. I also had to ask for help from others—more than once. But my vision exercises helped me control my life and live it on my owns terms. I can now recover from setbacks faster. I garner greater respect from my peers, especially from other Visionnaires who can see I am a member of their elite group. On top of that, I am presented with more opportunities, which, in turn, allow me to show other Visionnaires the value of my RFE and how it can help them with their own vision to reality roadmap.

Chapter 23:

PLANNING

Warren Buffet stated so eloquently that "an idiot with a plan can beat a genius without a plan." I agree with this as my success can be attributed to both my experience and my desire for a good plan. Plan for today. Plan for tomorrow. Be specific.

In my years of experience, I have learned the importance of planning—not only an overarching long-term plan but a plan for each day. I plan daily, for today and for tomorrow. My plans are specific and detailed, a part of my daily life. My calendar has two entries for each day. The first entry is what I plan for the next day. By the end of the day, I should have completed everything that I planned to do and take stock of anything that remains. However, the next day must also be set up for what I am going to do. When I adopted this, I started sleeping better at night. I don't worry when something doesn't get done because I have a plan for when I am going to take care of it. The second entry is scheduling something that allows me to learn something different in pursuit of my overall life goals. This is a simple reminder that in addition to running a business or working for someone, I have my own personal goals, and to meet these ambitious goals, I do something every day toward that goal.

I talk to entrepreneurs about planning every day. It doesn't matter if you already had your weekly meeting with the team. As an entrepreneur, you need to plan what you are going to do each day clearly with a high degree of focus on the tasks that matter. What did you accomplish yesterday? How can you make today better? What will your focus be tomorrow? You must continually be in a planning mindset. When you prepare and you plan ahead, you perform better.

The fact is, you cannot fix what you do not measure. Below is an example from the 2014 to 2016 Jenkins & Associates, Inc.'s goals.

The Vision/Goal: Grow Jenkins & Associates to a multi-million-dollar business in two years with a minimum of ten employees (project managers and office personnel).

To get to the vision/goal, I needed to create a plan to prospect and gain new customers and clients. For everything I do, there is a plan. Prior to hiring the sales team members, I developed a sales profile and worked with my network to help me source the sales team. Having the plan was helpful in providing clarity on the goals and steps to achieve the vision. The plan was simple:

1. Create tiered levels of employees with specific rates associated with each tier level. It helps to forecast revenue and pricing.
2. Provide the sales team with revenue targets and a commission schedule.
3. Provide guidance on where to find prospects for current business and new business.

Below is an example of the initial schedule I laid out for the sales team, which showed a potential of $2.6 million, although the goal was only to get above $1 million. The highest I achieved was $1.5 million, but in subsequent years I had to let go of the sourcing business because the market was too competitive, too time-consuming and not in line with my focus on strategic development. I learned to manage costs and negotiate to achieve better profit margins. Although the business did not end up being sustainable for me, my intention is to show how I started with planning. I was shooting for the moon and reached the stars.

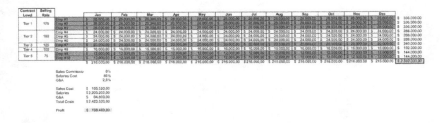

Encourage your team as they implement the plan, reminding them every step of the way that perfection is the enemy of progress. The 80 percent will make you richer than when you factor in the time and cost it would take to achieve the 100 percent. This is a simple, but effective, planning method that I have been using for a long time. It is easy to understand, and it outlines simplistic targets for salespeople.

Chapter 24:

GUIDE DAILY

You are the entrepreneur. The company is your business. As the leader, you must run meetings and guide your team on a daily basis. That's right: on a daily basis. You can't just send emails and hope to communicate your message well. If you don't make time to communicate well, you are setting your business up to fail. Spend more time with your team, guiding them daily. Your communication with them sets the tone for their communication with others, especially your other employees and, most importantly, your customers.

Communicating and Guiding the Team to Success

You are the leader. You are the Visionnaire. You are the one who sets the tone for the business, the attitude of the business, and the direction for the business. To communicate and guide your team to success, you must develop a strong rapport with your team. It is important to do whatever you must to build a solid, trusting relationship with your team. That relationship comes from having open, honest communication with each other. It comes from getting their input on how to make improvements in the workflow, in the business, and in serving customers and clients.

In daily practice, how do you work with them to develop a plan for communication? For employees who directly report to you, you should meet with them individually on a weekly basis. When you meet, remember this is their time one-on-one with you to work on not only what they understand as their place in the company, but also what they want for their careers and their goals. It is also their opportunity to ask you about the state of the business. It is your opportunity to be open and honest with each of them about what you are trying to achieve with the company, as well as what you expect from them. A failed relationship comes from failed expectations. Developing a rapport and realistic expectations with your people is invaluable.

In addition, have a weekly meeting with the whole team. Rally the troops and get them behind you. One of the things that multilevel marketing groups do well is rally the troops, bringing them together and selling the dream. This is also an effective method to get the most out of your people. Keep everyone updated on the status of the business with monthly calls, providing a message about the state of the organization. Share everything that is happening, the team's wins, and adjustments that need to be made. Do this regularly alongside the daily, weekly, monthly, and quarterly plans (as demonstrated below), showing who is expected to perform what duties on what cadence.

For example, let's explore business development opportunities. Business development occurs daily. Business owners must do everything necessary to keep the business viable. The company leaders can then focus on deliverables for their functions, driving direct reports, and discussing any issues or support that is required. Employees can execute their tasks from the weekly sales and operations plan and provide company leaders with updates on immediate issues.

Call this out and do it on a daily basis. Look at the daily, weekly, monthly, and quarterly activities, along with annual activities. This can serve as an overall communication plan and set expectations for the team clearly. Start doing this on a daily basis and it will become habit.

When you begin, it will not likely feel as organized as it appears on the chart below, but it will improve as you repeat the process daily, weekly, monthly, and quarterly and watch your business grow.

Below is an example of actions that may need to be taken by key stakeholders in the business. As you can see, everyone has a role in ensuring the business has continuity. Everyone is working together each day to drive the business toward its vision. Of course, these actions can be adjusted for your business, but this serves as a guide for how to bring everyone together on a regular basis. You can also add to the participants. For example, instead of just owners, company leaders, and employees, you can add board members, partners, etc. This is a great tool for communicating your intentions with the entire organization both internally and externally, and it can be updated frequently until all elements serve to build the business.

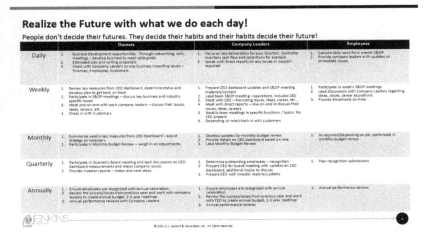

Communicating and guiding the team translates into serving customers and clients successfully. Excellent communication skills are crucial in the growth and operation of your business. When you optimize communication with your team, they, in turn, can do the same with your customers, which translates into more loyal customers and more revenue for your company.

Chapter 25:

ELEMENTS

Each entrepreneur must design a daily, weekly, monthly, and quarterly planning sheet with elements that fit their business model. Every business will be different. Each one has unique needs that must be met on a daily, weekly, monthly, and quarterly schedule. The elements on the planning sheet should be communicated well and should be clear to both you and your employees. Planning must include deliberate daily meetings with staff, sales and operations planning, meetings with the board of directors, and meetings with key divisions of your team (sales team, operations team, etc.)

Below is a sample analysis of an actual client's operations, meeting overviews, and planning.

Analysis of Operation

The Complaint:
The CEO wanted to fire the office manager because he felt the office manager was not doing what was needed to collect receivables. The CEO further stated that the office manager was not performing their duties adequately to allow the CEO to spend enough time on business development.

My Findings

[CEO Name],

Thank you for allowing me to share my experience and expertise on getting things done. I see you have a couple of key factors on which you need to focus so your business can be more successful. You need human resources practices in place to develop your talent, and you need to increase your focus on leadership—not "boss-ship" but leadership. I can help you put these practices in place. Here is the summary of my visit with [Office Manager] on 12/20/2019 from 9 a.m. to 12 p.m. To set the tone for this report, let me first state that the very basis of business is to manage three areas very well:

1. Cash Flow
2. Customers
3. Employees

Cash Flow

You stated that accounts receivable (AR) is one of your biggest challenges. I had [Office Manager] provide me with a statement from your Quick-Books's outstanding AR. I calculated a total of $324,000 in AR.

- $205,000 – Commercial
- $24,400 – Residential
- $52,900 – Unsure ([Office Manager] could not determine whether these were commercial accounts or residential accounts)

Additional breakdown of AR – largest groups owing [the company] are as follows:

1. Construction Company = $237,000
2. Storage Company = $66,000
3. EAGA = $9,500 (in collections)
4. DVR = $9,000 (in collections)

Recommendations to better manage cash flow:

1. The aging of the AR should be noted so we can determine the likelihood of capturing the AR. The longer the AR, i.e., above ninety days, the less likely it is to be collected. I had [Office Manager] work with me to create a spreadsheet in Microsoft Excel, and this needs to be regularly updated to prevent accounts from going to greater than thirty days outstanding for all commercial accounts and greater than three days for residential accounts.

2. I recommend that you invest in POS technology, perhaps an iPad with Square or something similar to collect payment when jobs are completed. I recently had service from Roto Rooter due to a plumbing leak and a heating contractor visit. They left my house when the job was done **paid in full.** You must implement this immediately to reduce the back-end strain of collecting your hard-earned payments. I am sure there will be exceptions, but that is exactly what it must be: an exception!

3. Your QuickBooks should be set up to produce this same report I was sent, and this report should be reviewed weekly with the team, [Office Manager], or whoever focuses on this process. Let us determine if we can resolve this or get some help, but this process is a must.

Customers

I do not have any recommendations here. You treat your customers very well. I would like to meet with you to discuss marketing to your customers, including social media opportunities. What do you want to get out of this? You treat your customers well. Our goal is to get your customers to treat you well by paying on time for your services.

Employees

This is your greatest challenge second only to cash flow, but it is an area of concern that can be resolved. However, this is a two-way street and will represent the most strain for you as a business owner and leader, and it is paramount to your success. In speaking with [Office Manager], here are the areas that must improve to get better results:

- Communication
- Planning
- Trust
- Training/Upskilling/Technology

Findings and Recommendations

You will have to be more present to communicate your desires. Each human has a need to communicate in ways they understand. I have run thousands of projects, large and small, and the number-one item that arises, both good and bad, is communication. Even the best projects I have run still had someone—some group, some region—I felt could have communicated better.

Also, I asked [Office Manager] what your 2019 Goals are, and she didn't know. This is a test I always ask every employee. Good organizations make sure their team members are fluent in the overall goals of the organization and, in turn, their individual goals tie into the organization's goals.

[Office Manager] and all team members must know your goals since they are, in reality, their goals as well. You must communicate the goals every opportunity you can. All goals may not need to include monetary goals, but the monetary goals are the results of your team's goals. We should get together and talk about your attrition goals (you want to keep people), industry and market goals, and individual goals. You need to know what your employees want to accomplish and then tie their goals into your goals.

Planning is key to success. I believe you meet with the team monthly. You will likely need to meet with [Office Manager] daily, but at least increase to weekly meetings for now. You are not micromanaging in doing so as much as conveying the message that she (or whoever you have as an office manager) is your partner. Thirty-minute huddle meetings, even on the phone, are hugely important for team success. The typical agenda quickly discusses the previous day's or week's accomplishments to set a good tone, then the issues encountered and the plan to resolve them, and what needs to be accomplished the next day or week. Doing so gets you and your team into a good rhythm for having a strong business relationship. During these meetings, you should cover:

Sales and Marketing Prospects
1. An update on performance: How did we do against our goal?
2. Goals for the week, month, and quarter
3. Plan of action (ask the team their plan) to reach these goals and how they can help: cold calls, social media, collections, etc.

Customers
1. Any customer complaints/issues?
2. What are they and how do we resolve the immediate issue?
3. How do we prevent these issues from occurring with other customers, i.e., what did we learn?

Employees
1. Quick forum: anything you have to say? Anything you need to be successful today/this week?
2. Any employee announcements/expectations

When it comes to trust, you are lucky, although you do not feel this way. You have one of the most loyal people I have ever met. I am just going to be blunt here. Let [Office Manager] take the [company] phone home. You already have cameras so you can watch people, and it does not feel good. She did not mention the cameras, but I remember it was an issue before with [Previous Office Manager]. All she wants and needs is to be trusted. She is loyal to a fault, and you will not find people like her easily.

[Office Manager] needs training and upskilling. This may be where you have some issues, but this can be fixed. I suggest she get some training on Microsoft Excel and Microsoft Word. She can use YouTube as a guide so this does not have to cost anything, but I think her development plan (something that needs to be put in place perhaps by a leader who is serving as HR) should have these elements in 2020. This will improve her confidence and pay great dividends to you.

Here are my recommendations for technology updates:

1. **POS** for collecting cash immediately – Square, iPad, etc.
2. **Electronic Signature** so you do not have to be present. My team has my e-signature to speed things up.
3. **Microsoft Office** upgrade and perhaps new computers/laptops or mobile device. You do not have to do this immediately, but the technology is so old that I need training.
4. **QuickBooks** reports that you can easily give to your office manager to take specific actions on, like AR aging.

Finally, I do not believe you need a new office manager. If you manage the same way, you will lose her. The younger workforce, in my experience, needs a great deal of attention and patting on the back for little to no work or effort. There was a recent study that showed you need to recognize your team members every seven days. Who has time for that? They are more tech-savvy and more social-media-savvy, but my recommendation is that you outsource certain work as projects to supplement the areas [Office Manager] is not well-versed in.

For example, we could have Upwork (someone in another country at $10 per hour) make calls for you to collect money. If you have a social media campaign, you can do the same thing. You contract out the projects, get them done, and move on.

We should also discuss your activities. We should look at which non-value-add activities we can get off your plate. I understand that the mailings are done exclusively by you. This should be delegated. What else should you delegate?

Let's get together and discuss. I will set aside some time to get you up and running for the year by working with you for the next couple of months. Before the new year, we should put together a 2020 plan.

***

After I provided this write-up, we got together and developed a plan for daily, weekly, monthly, quarterly, and annual engagement. Below is what that looked like for the weekly meeting with the framework we developed.

[Company] – Weekly Meeting

Agenda: Week of [date]

Employee Concerns:

- Company Updates – CEO, HR Leader
    a. expectations
    b. recognition
    c. mandatory meetings
    d. policies
    e. announcements
    f. anything else you need employees to know or do
- Customer Concerns – Team
    a. Customer issues/complaints – plan of action to resolve (what, when, who)

   b. Customer success stories
- Acknowledgments
- Testimonials
- Business – CEO
   a. $324,000 in AR, goal is to collect 50 percent by end of week
- Office Manager Goal
- CEO Goal
- HR Leader goal
- Goals for collection agency
   b. Sales goal for week (Should be a breakdown of yearly goal into a week)
- Goal/50)
   c. Week over week comparison for AR and sales goals. How did we do? What do we need to do better in? What did we learn? Please focus on identifying a solution to the problem.
- Roundtable – Give each person an opportunity to speak. Call their names out – any questions, issues, concerns, items to share?
- End of Meeting – Review all the action items (should be captured by office manager). End positively, driving team toward a sense of urgency, praise where necessary, admonish as a way of motivation, and express gratitude for having a great team. Lead by positive example.

Prep for meeting (Friday to Sunday). Get report from office manager (due by Friday afternoon or Thursday afternoon depending on her work schedule). It should include the action items and status of the week's goals, your notes, and hers, including updates in each category. Pull AR and sales reports from the past week and compare them to the goals, prepare your message about goals (positive and negative), and set next week's goals.

For this client, this was the guide we developed to maintain their business operations on a daily to annual basis:

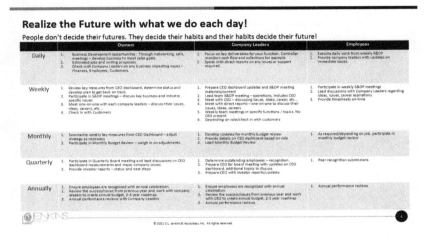

Realize the Future with what we do each day!
People don't decide their futures. They decide their habits and their habits decide their future!

	Owners	Company Leaders	Employees
Daily	1. Business Development opportunities: Through networking, calls, meetings – develop business to meet sales goals. 2. Estimated jobs and writing proposals. 3. Check with Company Leaders on any business impacting issues – Finances, Employees, Customers.	1. Focus on key deliverables for your function. Controller monitors cash flow and collections for example 2. Speak with direct reports on any issues or support required.	1. Execute daily work from weekly S&OP 2. Provide company leaders with updates on immediate issues.
Weekly	1. Review key measures from CEO dashboard, determine status and develop plan to get back on track. 2. Participate in S&OP meetings – discuss key business and industry specific issues 3. Meet one-on-one with each company leaders – discuss their issues, ideas, careers, etc... 4. Check in with Customers	1. Prepare CEO dashboard updates and S&OP meeting materials/content 2. Lead team S&OP meeting – operations, includes CEO 3. Meet with CEO – discussing issues, ideas, career, etc... 4. Meet with direct reports – one-on-one to discuss their issues, ideas, careers. 5. Weekly team meetings in specific functions / topics. No CEO present 6. Depending on role/check in with customers	1. Participate in weekly S&OP meetings 2. Lead discussions with Company Leaders regarding ideas, issues, career aspirations. 3. Provide timesheets on-time
Monthly	1. Summarize weekly key measures from CEO Dashboard – adjust strategy as necessary 2. Participate in Monthly Budget Review – weigh in on adjustments.	1. Develop updates for monthly budget review. 2. Provide details on CEO dashboard based on role 3. Lead Monthly Budget Review	1. As required/depending on job, participate in monthly budget review
Quarterly	1. Participate in Quarterly Board meeting and lead discussions on CEO dashboard measurements and major company issues. 2. Provide investor reports – status and next steps	1. Determine outstanding employees – recognition. 2. Prepare CEO for board meeting with updates on CEO dashboard, additional topics to discuss. 3. Prepare CEO with investor reports/updates	1. Peer recognition submissions
Annually	1. Ensure employees are recognized with annual celebration. 2. Review the success/issues from previous year and work with company leaders to create annual budget, 2-3 year roadmap 3. Annual performance reviews with Company Leaders	1. Ensure employees are recognized with annual celebration. 2. Review the success/issues from previous year and work with CEO to create annual budget, 2-3 year roadmap 3. Annual performance reviews	1. Annual performance reviews

The example above focuses on the weekly sales and operations planning for this business. I also created a monthly milestones chart to support these activities that can be used as a reminder for the owner of what needs to be in place and executed—preventing backsliding.

As an example, the monthly milestones chart looks like this:

Realize the Future with what we do each day!
People don't decide their futures. They decide their habits and their habits decide their future!

	Owners	Company Leaders	Employees
Daily	1. 2 Hours! Plan and execute Business Development opportunities: Through networking, calls, meetings – develop business to meet sales goals. 2. 30 Minutes! 7:00am – Check with Office Manager on: Daily Tasks required, Customers, Issues, Call Outs, etc... 3. 2 Hours! Estimate jobs and writing proposals. 4. 1 Hour! Plan for next day – determine what's the most important item that requires attention	1. Execute daily work prioritized by Owner – operations and towards strategy 2. Provide updates to owner with agreed upon frequency 3. Communicate with field personnel as required 4. Communicate with customers as required	1. Execute daily work from Planning meetings 2. Provide Office Manager and Owner with updates on immediate issues 3. Collect cash on all completed jobs - immediately
Weekly	1. Monday Morning: 5 am: Review key measures from CEO dashboard and office manager report. Determine status and develop plan to get back on track 2. Monday morning: 7:00am: Lead weekly Planning meeting – Business updates, Sales & marketing, Customer concerns, Employee concerns, Actions to take this week, reiterate vision and goals 3. Meet with Office Manager and employees regarding their specific needs and concerns. No more than 30 minutes – Listen to them	1. Prepare CEO dashboard updates and weekly meeting materials/content 2. Meet with Owner – discussing issues, ideas, career, etc...	1. Participate in weekly planning meetings 2. Lead discussions with Owner regarding ideas, issues, career aspirations. 3. Provide timesheets on-time
Monthly	1. First week after month end: Summarize weekly key measures from CEO Dashboard – adjust strategy as necessary towards vision 2. First week after month end: Monthly Budget Review with Office Manager – weigh in on adjustments.	1. Develop updates for monthly budget review. 2. Provide details for CEO dashboard	1. As required/depending on job, participate in monthly budget review
Quarterly	1. Participate in Quarterly Board meeting and lead discussions on CEO dashboard measurements and major company issues. 2. Work with Office Manager and accountant to develop financial reports in preparation for advisory board meeting	1. Determine outstanding employees – recognition. 2. Prepare Owner for board meeting with updates on CEO dashboard, additional topics to discuss. 3. Take meeting minutes for quarterly board meeting 4. Send Board meeting communications as directed	1. Peer recognition submissions
Annually	1. Ensure employees are recognized with annual celebration. 2. Review the success/issues from previous year and work with Office manager and accountant to create annual budget, 2-3 year roadmap 3. Annual performance reviews with Office Manager and Employees	1. Help Owner perform recognition celebration activities. 2. Annual performance review	1. Annual performance reviews

As you can see, the continuation of the daily, weekly, monthly, quarterly, and annual activities roll into these milestones with a quarterly view. This is just another snapshot of the plan entrepreneurs can follow to keep from backsliding and develop the habits and actions they need to stay on track.

Chapter 26:

DEVELOPING MUSCLE

N o matter how taxing it may seem, entrepreneurs must spend time developing their muscles. And when I say taxing, it really is. You must develop your muscles as an entrepreneur—your mental muscles, that is. It is an ongoing process that will continue throughout your career. You must retrain your mind. You must spend time with your team and your customers. You must focus on the people—customers and employees—spending your time, money, and energy on them. Spending that time with your people allows you to duplicate yourself and thus duplicate your business.

Trust in the development process as you fail up. It is how life works—filled with failures and successes. The key to developing your muscles whenever you fail is failing up. Every failure is an opportunity to learn. Every setback is also an opportunity. You must develop those muscles and understand that failing up is better than doing nothing.

There are three major elements that I use to ensure I build muscle and prevent backsliding: Habits (Systems), Measurements (Key Performance Indicators), and Accountability (Advisors and Mentors).

Use Systems

The development of muscles comes from this process. You have to define a goal, execute the goal, and create a system to maintain the goal. For example, most people have experienced setting the goal to lose weight. It begins with the creation of an initial goal. Let's say you want to lose twenty pounds. Next, we set out to execute the goal, performing all the actions we know like eating less and exercising more. We hit our goal weight, but six months later, we see we have regained the weight and don't understand why. We then set another goal and repeat this cycle until we give up.

Or we change our lifestyle with the systems needed to maintain the goal weight.

The systemic approach is so much better than cycling through the never-ending repetition. We change the goal to say we want a healthy lifestyle that allows us to fit into our favorite clothes. To do this, the statement changes to something like: "I need to remain a size X. I'd like to ensure I have no other underlying conditions, so I measure my blood pressure, blood sugar, etc."

The system then becomes:

- Run two miles per day
- Prepare and eat foods that do not have a high sugar content
- Journal what you eat each day
- Measure your blood pressure and blood sugar daily

Once you spend thirty to forty-five days doing this, suddenly it becomes a lifestyle for you. You see when you are not doing as well, when your numbers are not improving. I personally did this to lose over seventeen pounds and took my blood sugar reading from a diabetic 233 to a regular reading of one hundred over a period of five months. Whenever I overdo eating or drinking, my measurements tell me I need to readjust by getting back to my healthy lifestyle immediately.

This is the same way I approach business with my business partners. We develop systems of habits and measure them daily, weekly, and monthly. In one instance, I was working with a client and we had just started our cash flow meetings when the client confessed that he felt as though he was being beat up because he was not performing to the measures we set out initially. DSO was up to three weeks and cash was either high or very low (in some cases even negative with bank fees). Working on just the DSO and performing a weekly cash flow review with all the business leaders led to a steady increase in the bank account and the ability to pay bills.

I finally got to the bottom of the issue when I received a call in the middle of the week from the owner confessing that he hated the process because he felt exposed and everyone was pointing fingers saying he was the reason the business was failing. What actually happened was they all learned how important DSO was and dividing the labor and having someone else focus on collections was the answer.

However, after six weeks of doing this and showing vast improvement, the owner became distracted with life (he and his wife had a baby), and we immediately went back to a negative bank balance in just two weeks. This really exposed the need to have someone else focus on doing the collections, create a robust POS system, and keep DSO to less than three days. We immediately recovered and never looked back.

I had encouraged the other leaders in the company, in a separate discussion, to institute positive praise for achievements to reinforce the owner's behavior. The new system was put in place, and we changed our focus to business development and growth.

As the leader of your organization, you must recognize that these systems are key for your success. In implementing systems, you can also train yourself to work with your team members, customers, and potential customers, along with any other relationships necessary to keep your business growing.

Use Measurements

In the above example, I focused on systems, but inherent in the system are the key measures needed to drive the business forward. For the issue of not collecting cash, the measurement was DSO. It was the key measure to ensure that the business became—and remained—cash flow positive. Measures should be put in place anywhere your business is having issues that must be corrected. As I outlined earlier, I like to have four major areas for measurements: Financial Measures, Employee Measures, Customer Measures, and Sales Measures.

Money is the lifeblood of the company. Its flow—or lack of flow—is like our bodies pumping blood. If it has a positive flow where more money is coming in then going out, we have a healthy business. If its flow is negative, that is a recipe for disaster for both the person and the business. The major elements of financial health that I use are working capital, gross profit, EBITDA, and free cash. There are additional financial measures that can be used, but I find that with small businesses, these measures are the most important for determining the status and direction of the company.

I find that small businesses are not measuring employees except by logging mental frustration when employees are not performing to their expectations. In my experience, this is a direct result of owners not spending enough time with their employees to develop a bidirectional rapport in growing the business. I ask them to first record the amount of time they spend with the employee, measure their progress on achieving their goals, and measure the opportunities and recognition given to employees. You may think, who has time for recognition? But if you focus on what you can do to help employees be successful, your return on your time and the results of your business will be a tremendous gain. The way to do this is not to put an actual measure in place but to put the day/time you spend with them on the calendar and focus on them, their development, and their suggestions for improving the company. Give them your full attention. You will see that this simple system of a weekly, one-on-one engagement will produce tremendous results and grow their loyalty, and loyalty is immeasurable.

This same approach to measurement can be used with customers. I have my business partners note the last time they engaged a customer. Based on the business type, I encourage them to look for ways to engage the customer again through a phone call, email, referral request, etc. You can measure how much business a particular customer has helped you with, and you can reward them. This will certainly create a client who is loyal to you and help you grow your business.

Finally, for sales measures, I use simple measurements that line up with the overall revenue goals of the organization. Depending on your business, I like to tie customer measurements and sales measurements together with a CRM system to easily measure the effectiveness of customer and sales performance by customer.

Implementing a CRM System

Using a CRM system such as Saleforce can help you tremendously.

For larger companies, a CRM system can easily manage existing and potential customer interaction to help businesses build relationships while increasing sales and profitability alongside improving customer service. For smaller companies, I develop a simple spreadsheet the office manager or administrative assistant uses to schedule and record interactions with customers. It can also have space to log customer complaints and returns to analyze trends that can either be resolved simply or require a visit with the customer immediately to address a problem.

When the company grows sufficiently, it is time to move from a simple spreadsheet to a custom CRM system. Companies both large and small can leverage a CRM system for the benefit of their business, keeping in mind that the goal of any CRM—from a simple spreadsheet to a custom CRM system—is to enhance a company's relationship with clients, customers, and prospects. Just like the spreadsheet system I use with my business partners at the beginning of their journey, a CRM is a tool designed to gather, organize, and manage customer information while simplifying their operations.

One of the advantages a CRM system can offer a growing company of any size is customer retention. As you know, when prospects and customers are converted to clients who keep coming back for more of your products or services, increased revenue often results. CRM systems use strategies to help you retain clients by encouraging repeat business, supplying information to customers, and building relationships to develop satisfied customers.

In addition, because it stores your customer data in centralized area, a custom CRM system allows you to gain valuable insights into your company's overall performance. From lead generation to marketing campaign results to revenue generation totals, a CRM can allow you to see company performance, your wins, and your losses, so you can make adjustments, improve operations, and increase your revenue.

A personalized CRM system can also help your business improve customer satisfaction. Within a CRM, your data is so organized that it is easy to understand your customers and identify their pain points, enabling you to better serve them. Using your CRM system effectively, you and your employees will know when a customer has a problem, and because you have all the information you need at your fingertips, your company can quickly provide a solution. Customer feedback is ongoing with a CRM system, which allows you to continually improve your customer service and, in turn, customer satisfaction.

Not only does a custom CRM system improve customer relations but it can also enhance the communication and performance of your team members. As a business tool, your CRM allows company and customer data to be easily shared. As a result, processes are optimized, improving efficiency and production. Your CRM allows your employees to improve their performance levels by providing crucial customer information for team members to effectively offer premium products, upgrades, and complementary products.

Finally, a custom CRM system allows you to target your marketing efforts more effectively. By analyzing customer groups from the data, your marketing efforts can be optimized to reach more prospects, convert them to customers, and then convert them to clients, thereby increasing your sales and earning greater profits.

Interacting with Mentors/Advisors

Finally, a system of accountability is a must-have as you are developing your muscles. First, no one ever succeeds alone, and as I discuss throughout the book, one of the key elements to success is the people in the business ecosystem. And a key relationship that requires frequent interaction is the one with your mentor or advisors. They should help you brainstorm ideas, clear the fog on issues you may be facing, and act as a sounding board when you need to vent frustrations. You cannot measure the amount of time saved because someone who has been there before you steers you away from imminent trouble or helps streamline a course of action through relationships or tried-and-true approaches. Having a mentor or advisor is priceless. If you don't have one, I suggest you begin the process of finding one in your network or through engagement in trade associations, etc. One of my business partners had the goal to seek a mentor, and I helped them create a statement to articulate the company, its purpose, and its goals, including the desire to have a mentor.

Spending the necessary quality time with these key individuals, team members, customers, and advisors on a scheduled basis will help you improve as a leader and will have a significant improvement on the business while you develop your mental muscles.

Chapter 27:

FINANCIAL PERSPECTIVE

D isclaimer: I am not a financial professional. My advice is based on my experiences as a project manager and as an investor. I employ professionals to help me financially to plan and execute. Now, with that out of the way, I wanted to make sure I provided some insight on financial perspective in this book. I started working with small businesses when people in my network started coming to me for financial advice or to ask for money as an investment to help grow their businesses. I found that many of these business owners did not need money or didn't know how much they needed. They wanted money but did not want to give up control of their business or gain a ridiculous interest rate. They had exhausted their means of getting money (credit cards, bank loans, loans against assets, friends, and family, etc.) They were constantly living payroll to payroll. This was not to the case with all clients, but the ones who asked for money really just needed an education on money, the right financial partners and support, and the right employees to ensure that money was collected and reported properly.

According to research on why small businesses fail, 82 percent of small businesses fail due to issues with cash flow. The best entrepreneurs understand business from a financial perspective: cash flow, COGS (costs of goods sold), gross margins, EBITDA, and more. Those who don't understand their business by the numbers are those who get into issues with their business.

The Number-One Problem is Knowing Your Cash Flow

I recently did a survey of entrepreneurs about raising capital. I asked what the top three problems they faced were. The number-one problem was consistently lack of capital or lack of access to capital.

Investment capital is critical to support an entrepreneur's capacity to create new jobs and additional wealth, yet it seems to be always out of reach for entrepreneurs. There could be any number of reasons why. In my experience, entrepreneurs do not examine the reason they need capital nor do they know how much capital they need, and they take Band-Aid approaches. For example, they borrow from friends and family or borrow from banks early on without a clear plan for the best way to use the funds. These are risky behaviors that make them a credit risk, which in turn makes it difficult for them to borrow from banks in the future. They don't understand the language that will show investors they have a viable business. So, with this big issue—their lack of cash flow—they fail to meet any lender's standard loan benchmarks. Bank regulators rely on these standards, which makes it difficult for businesses to get loans.

One of the biggest reasons they fail to meet the standard loan benchmarks is many entrepreneurs lack the financial records, which creates a big barrier. It is difficult to get lenders to provide much-needed support during negative economic conditions, such as a recession, without financial records. In the pandemic of 2020, there was one area in which the government was giving away money for free, but the process was so bad that many small businesses were hurt, and the big businesses got more money than they needed.

Paperwork can seem like an insurmountable barrier to qualify for banking, bank loans, or investors. It is difficult to create a strategic relationship with a bank, though it is good to have one. One of the areas I work with my business partners on is getting a controller, not just a bookkeeper. You need a controller who has experience with financing. You may even want a finance professional if you can afford it. The first loan I recommend is one designed to pay for the working capital to move your business forward. It should include the funds you need for a controller if you don't have one. Clean paperwork with the right financial measures shows you are a viable business, and you become less of a risk to banks when applying for any future loans.

Most of what people need money for is working capital and investment capital for expansion. In my experience, no one has asked me to help them get investment capital for expansion; they were always asking for working capital so they could make payroll and meet other expenses to continue to operate their businesses. This is especially true for businesses where customers require a long lead time to pay for services. You need clean financial records to project cash flow and visualize when money is coming and going, which you need when you seek loans from banks.

So, small businesses need sufficient financial records, including smart business plans and solid market research on the business, in order to raise capital. Healthy cash flow is critical to securing a loan. You have to know your numbers. You must have clean records. You have to understand your industry. You must have the right people in place to help you, or you will not be able to secure the necessary capital from banks or investors. In both cases, they want to know how much you need, how you will use the funds, and when they will be paid back with accumulated interest.

Defining Finances and Key Measures

Understanding key financials is paramount to success. Below are the areas in which every entrepreneur should be well-versed.

Working Capital

By definition, working capital is the capital available to your business for day-to-day use. It is most simply calculated by subtracting current liabilities from current assets. In order to operate a business, the flow of money in and out of the business must be managed well.

The goal is to have the income coming to you faster than money is going out for expenses. To measure this for my business partners, I use the formulas for DSO and DPO.

DSO = Accounts Receivables / Net Credit Sales X Number of Days
DPO = Accounts Payable / (Cost of Sales / Number of days)

When your work is completed for a client, the goal is to get payment as quickly as possible. I usually advise my service clients to collect no more than three days after the service was provided. I really prefer collection in full on the same day as project completion, but some owners want to provide a final inspection of their work for their customers.

On the flip side, I advise customers to pay their expenses with five days after the expense is due when they can do so without penalty. If rent is due on the first of the month, I advise them to pay the rent on the fifth or sixth. Waiting five days will not hurt the company while the company is collecting more money. It will also not damage their credit or relationships.

In some cases, payment must be done on time, but the goal is to collect quick and pay slow. You can get an early read on your cash flow if the DSO number of days is not hitting your targets. This is an easy red flag for the entrepreneur to measure. If you don't get ahead of this, you will feel the pain when you are scrambling to pay bills, including payroll, because you don't have the cash. Having a line of credit helps, but it is better for a business to self-fund expenses and use a line of credit for growing the business versus maintaining the business. Remember, credit comes with a cost. There is no return on investment when paying bills with credit.

Gross Margin or Gross Profit

Gross margin is defined as a company's net sales less its COGS. Essentially, gross margin or gross profit is just that: the gross sales revenue after subtracting the costs associated with the services provided or production of the items being sold. To calculate gross margin or profit, you use the income in any given period less the costs associated with creating or delivering the product or service.

Cost of Goods Sold

The COGS includes the direct labor used to create or deliver the service, materials directly related to the product or service, and equipment for the product or service creation or delivery. This measure tells you if you are consistent in your costs against the income. It also helps you determine if you are getting a reasonable price for your service or product. To measure this, you must research your industry to determine if your gross margin or gross profit percentages are equal, higher, or lower the average in your industry.

For example, if an industry comparison of four or five companies reveals you have a gross margin of 30 percent, that is your COGS, which accounts for 70 percent of your income. If your industry analysis showed your peer companies have a gross margin of 40 percent, you would need to make some adjustments to get a better profit margin. You can always raise prices to increase the income. While this may have a negative effect on your customers' willingness to do business with you, it will help you if you've determined that you may be underpriced in the market.

Another way to increase gross margin or profit is to lower your costs associated with the product or service created or delivered. You can use cheaper labor, which may have some consequences, or you can find cheaper materials or develop an innovation that automates part of your delivery system and drives down costs.

For one client, I advised that the company add 3 percent to their costs to cover merchant fees. I also recommended the company add tax

(4 percent in their state) to the invoice. Their customers could easily understand the specific costs versus an overall price increase.

Every situation is different, but you want to measure the financial factors so you know what and how you can improve. Big companies do these analyses on a regular basis and make adjustments to steer the company in the right direction.

EBITDA

The next measure of financial health is earnings before income tax, depreciation, and amortization, also known as EBITDA. Another commonly used term for EBITDA is net income before taxes. After the gross margin or profit is calculated, the costs for selling and general administration must be factored in. These are your costs for overhead like the office expenses, rent, and salaries for individuals who are not direct labor but are needed to run the business, such as an office manager. This provides another measure on how well you are performing as a business. The calculation uses the same process of determining how good companies run well.

For example, a good EBITDA percentage is 20 percent. Simply stated, the net income before taxes is 20 percent of the overall income. Therefore, your selling and general administration costs were an additional 10 percent of your costs at 30 percent gross margin or 20 percent at 40 percent gross margin.

Either way, you can do your best to drive efficiencies in your business to lower these costs. Finding a less expensive location, upskilling your people to take on multiple roles, or reducing the number of employees are all good ways of reducing these costs. If you are measuring a number less than 10 percent, you can see that once you pay your taxes, debt, and other expenses, you won't have much left for investing (growing the business). These are a few of the most critical measures of cash flow to help a business to grow and maintain a healthy company.

Free Cash Flow

Finally, free cash flow (FCF) is another measure which gives you, as well as potential investors, an indication of your ability to manage the company from a financial perspective. Free cash flow is a measure of profitability as the cash a company generates after subtracting the outflows that support company operations and maintain company assets. It differs from net income (earnings) in that it excludes non-cash expenses, including equipment or asset spending.

Free cash flow provides a cushion for making significant decisions such as capital investments. For example, we can grow a fleet of trucks, buy a building, or make another major investment that provides a financial return to the business.

Most small businesses put their free cash into a reserve account, which is a good practice when it includes rules for how the reserve may be accessed.

Know Your Numbers

If you manage your cash flow horribly, it can get you into trouble. If you don't have a good relationship with your bank, the same is true. Your banker needs to know how your business is performing financially. To keep your banker informed, you need to know which measures make you look your best on paper. Business owners understand they must collect payments from customers to pay their debts, but if they don't know the working capital measures that determine whether their business is healthy, they will fall short of success.

If you, as an entrepreneur, don't understand your total cost of goods sold, you'll never be able to estimate a project correctly. In most instances, you'll underestimate, incorrectly calculating all your costs. The result is that you try to get the project done by not charging customers sufficiently, which from one job to the next is completely unmanageable. But, if you understand your costs, you can estimate project costs effectively, as well as communicate those costs to your customers. The goal is to always have quality goods and services, and while your clients are looking for a cost-effective value, they know the value of outstanding quality and service and are willing to pay more to get it.

The same is true for understanding your gross margin, profit margin, and all the other financial details that help you manage your business well by the numbers. Some try to get the sale and disregard their costs by developing pricing based on what they judge someone is willing to pay. Knowing your numbers and your value, you can feel confident you are asking for what you deserve and are willing to leave some business on the table instead of compromising your principles. Get professional help to learn the numbers required for your business.

Chapter 28:

STRENGTHEN THE VISION

The best entrepreneurs strengthen their vision and carry it through to success. For entrepreneurs, knowledge and communication are necessary to remove obstacles along the way, strengthen their vision, and carry on until the vision becomes a reality. Strengthening the vision means you keep moving forward, even when you don't feel like it. It means learning to recognize growth and follow through with the RFE, know that even when you can't see it working right away, the fog is clearing. It means planning effectively and guiding your team with exceptional communication and leadership—daily, weekly, and monthly. Strengthening the vision means failing up, using setbacks as opportunities to learn and build muscle. It means gaining a clear understanding of financials so you can adjust the vision as needed to achieve the reality you desire.

The Application of the Realization Framework Experience

The Realization Framework Experience is not a one-and-done activity. It is a series of activities and engagements between the leadership, the advisors, and the employees, as well as the customers and the suppliers of the company. To begin, the leadership must determine their vision, values, and strategic objectives.

If you are an entrepreneur or a business leader, it all begins with defining the problem you hope to solve and where you are trying to lead your company. Where do you want to go? What is the state of your business as you see it? What is the state of the business as you would like to see it? What is the vision?

In one instance, I discussed working with a company, but they decided they did not want to use the RFE. Later, the company was in a considerable amount of trouble. In fact, they were in crisis mode. I offered to work with them and help them get back on their feet. For them, the first objective was to get out of crisis mode. They had to see and understand what was actually happening within the company. The goal was to go from crisis mode to stabilization mode to transformation mode. Before I could allow the business leadership to focus on where they wanted to be, I needed them to focus on just being. They had to get out of their immediate debt, get past the inability to make payroll, get out of the how-to-rob-Peter-to-pay-Paul mode, and stop taking small loans from friends and family. They had to come to terms with the crisis and really understand what the problem was.

In working through the problem, we determined there was an issue with cash flow, which was essential since there was no understanding of cash flow in the company. Money was being spent because materials were needed, but no one ever bothered to ask if the company was collecting enough money to do so. Bank fees were off the charts, and desperation had kicked in.

Building a short-term cash flow plan for the first few weeks was the first step. It included showing *on paper* the gaps of income and restructuring jobs so that the flow of funds was steadier. A plan was developed to furlough employees because there was not enough capital or cash coming in to make payroll because they simply did not have enough work. Right-sizing the organization based on cash flow was priority one.

The second step was to analyze the types of jobs needed to bring in quick money. In this case, the answer was small maintenance jobs and residential jobs. From there, showing and developing a model and a process with the business leader and his partner allowed us to create a weekly cadence on just cash flow:

- How much money was in the bank
- How much money was to be collected
- What jobs were to be done
- What jobs were active
- How much payroll would be required for the coming weeks

Below is a snapshot of the information reviewed. Actual numbers are not provided for privacy reasons.

Q1 2021
Week Beginning

Beginning Bank Balance:

Planned Income:
Planned Costs:
Planned Profit/(Loss):

Actual Income:
Actual Costs:
Actual Profit/(Loss):

%Accuracy Income:

%Accuracy Costs:

We did this every week, looking ahead two weeks. We would measure how well we planned against how well we actually did. In the beginning, it was horrible. I knew it was not going to be a good session when I received the bank balance. I knew we would have some work to do. We would plan for an amount of income that made us feel comfortable, but we would not make it. The estimates seemed reasonable but always fell short. This is why we measure. The numbers do not lie. Showing this information looking back told the owner that they were really bad at estimating income and they had little to no control over expenses, which were flowing out faster than the income was coming in. My goal was to measure whether we were achieving 80 percent accuracy on income and costs. We started around 20 percent. Bills continued to pile on, along with bank fees.

The scramble continued, but slowly by gaining an understanding that cash collections is more important than the job itself, we crawled our way out of crisis mode to stabilization mode. This took two quarters (six months from crisis to stabilization). Then we could revisit the conversation about where they were trying to take the company.

Leadership indicated they were trying to take the company to a level of transformation. The company was at $1.2 million, and we built a plan for $5 million, $15 million, and $25 million over the next three years. We agreed we would need to segment into specific markets and put the leader into their area of strength (business development). From there, it was a matter of daily, weekly, monthly, quarterly, and annual activities and watching the business grow—and the company is still growing!

Leveraging the RFE—understanding financials, evaluating and adding the right personnel, including hiring a professional controller to help, hiring other resources who would handle the day-to-day operations, and having the leader partner with a large firm—contributed to the growth and success of this business. In addition, we developed clarity with a plan of risk mitigation and the plans for daily, weekly, monthly, quarterly, and annual activities. We also developed a what-if analysis to handle any issues like those that occurred during the pandemic. We developed a debt management and repayment plan. This company's issues stemmed purely from a negative financial situation. They had to recoup financially, but in rebuilding the company, we were able to get them on track to be like the model company they hoped to emulate.

One final act was that the company brought me on to lead their board of advisors. It is what I often do when working with an organization to build and strengthen the vision. In doing so, I continue to work with them not as a consultant but as an advisor to help them continue along the framework of the RFE methodology. It must be continued and built into the entire infrastructure to strengthen the vision. Follow the plan and build in accountability. I serve on the boards of many companies and help them plan, measure, adjust, and succeed.

Keep the Vision and the Reality Strong and Successful into the Future

Vision to Reality was written for business leaders and entrepreneurs who know their "Why?" but still need to understand the "how" to guide and grow their business successfully. The message of the book is simple, yet profound: clear the fog, develop the vision, and learn the skills to succeed in your business and industry. The RFE is designed to take you there, leveraging the expertise of my background in project management, operations, communication, and consultancy. The goal is to bring your vision to reality with my guidance and expertise, whether your business is large or small.

The truth is, the key components of success do not require a large cash position, and the RFE can take you to success in clear and concise steps. Through the challenges, the RFE is designed to take your business from vision to reality, a place of continued growth and success.

Are you ready to stop working so hard, stop living payroll to payroll, and start living the life you dreamed of? Take the Visionnaire Scorecard at https://visionnaire.scoreapp.com/ to get started and determine your strengths and opportunities in the *Vision to Reality* journey.

PART 4:
Case Studies

BDFS

GROUP

design - construction - renovation

Introduction

BDFS Group is a team of construction professionals founded in 2008 based in Philadelphia, PA. BDFS provides clients with top-quality services in residential and commercial projects of various sizes throughout the Greater Philadelphia area.

Problem

The company was seeking to expand their business. The company was growing fast but needed the structure, capital, and talent to meet demand. BDFS had the good problem of an explosion in business with back-loaded contracts that would be paid when the jobs were completed, but they did not have enough people or capital for supplies. Also, there was not a good structure with roles and responsibilities to divide and conquer, which had the owner focused too much on non-value-add work. To make matters worse, while we were in the beginning stages of restructuring the business, their largest client made the decision to fold their business. The hit to BDFS was a $600,000 non-payment that severely impacted their ability to keep the business afloat. The company began living paycheck to paycheck, scrambling to borrow money from various sources and spending many days and nights trying to keep the business afloat.

Actions

Jenkins & Associates helped organize the path to resolving this problem. First, we had to develop three phases of focus: crisis, stabilization, and transformation. At the beginning of our engagement, we were focused on transformation. This is where we looked at building the business to $25 million with BDFS's vision to be the largest minority-owned construction management and general contracting firm in Pennsylvania. However, we had to quickly pivot to crisis mode. The first thing we did was develop the fastest path to cash. I led an exercise to review the cash flow on a daily basis. The goal was to become cash flow positive as quickly as we could. We discovered that we had to do the following:

1. Focus on short-term residential work that pays immediately. Collect cash immediately after jobs are finished. They had an unbelievable number of accounts receivables.

2. Streamline talent with the best people who can finish jobs quickly.

3. Get rid of all non-value-add expenses and turn off all automated payments.

4. In addition to an unbelievable number of accounts receivables, they had an incredible number of accounts payables; therefore, we had to make deals with all suppliers to defer payments until we were cash flow positive.

5. Take on no additional work for which the client does not want to pay a 30 percent mobilization fee.

This crisis mode lasted for three months before we became cash flow positive. We kept weekly cash flow meetings to review and adjust activities until we became cash flow positive by measuring the accuracy of expected income and expenses until we reached 80 percent on a consistent basis. The RFE was used for steps two (evaluate your people), three (know your cash flow), and four (clear the fog) with a plan to execute. Once we were out of crisis mode, we began to look at the entire RFE, starting with the vision of being the largest minority contractor in Pennsylvania. Here are the steps we took:

- Developed a financial forecast based on the previous year's performance, adding growth to go from $1.2 million in the previous two years to $5 million in the first year, $10 million in the second year, and $25 million in the third year. We created a budget that supported the first year and had financial support to help us develop measures to know where we stood financially at all times. This was also to help the company position itself for a line of credit to help with larger jobs.

  - Target objectives included:

- ◆ AR: Collect money less than three days after a completed residential job and less than forty-five days commercial jobs
- ◆ AP: Add five days after invoice due to slow payments down.
- ◆ Daily sales targets of $14,000
- Found a company that we wanted to mirror: Turner Construction. Then we broke down the elements of Turner that we would mirror. Organization was the biggest thing to mirror, and we structured a plan to organize and hire people to match their organization from a roles and responsibilities perspective.
  - Hire four key personnel:
    - ◆ Controller – to help with keeping the financials clean and ensuring money is collected based on targets
    - ◆ Project Manager – to help remove work from owner
    - ◆ Assistant – to help owner with administration, customers, employees, etc.
    - ◆ Plumber – to keep owner from doing the plumbing portion of jobs and get his time back to work on business development.
- Developed a set of plans that included a risk mitigation plan and a strategic scenario plan to ensure a heightened awareness of anything that could derail the plan and how we would behave should a situation arise. Included in the plan were daily, weekly, monthly, quarterly, and annual activities that must be done by the owner, the new hires, the leaders, and the employees in the field.
- Jenkins & Associates provided their dashboard of measurements. That included financial measures, employee measures, customer measures, and sales measures.
- Finally, BDFS hired Jenkins & Associates as the chairman of their board to provide accountability for the agreed-upon actions

to meet the monthly targets. These were reviewed quarterly with the intention of adhering to or adjusting the measures to keep the company on its growth trajectory.

Outcome

BDFS is now thriving with the ability to complete all their jobs and a model that is flexible and ready for additional growth. Jenkins & Associates applied the elements of the RFE to help the company stabilize and obtain the necessary capital to begin the transformation portion of the engagement. This proves that before we need money, we need to organize for success, then determine the money, people, and plan that will get us from vision to reality!

Testimonials

"Jenkins & Associates helped us to organize for success to get our business out of crisis mode. I thought we were going to lose everything, but Curtis helped with seeing the areas that we needed to focus on. Communication with my business partner has vastly improved and now that I am focusing more on business development, I am able to obtain the jobs necessary to get to our goal of being the largest minority-owned business in Pennsylvania. I am glad that we consulted Curtis Jenkins as a committed partner to our success and will continue to leverage his experience to help us grow our business."
~ Calvin Snowden, CEO, BDFS

JUST IT'S ELECTRIC

Introduction

Just It's Electric is a full-service, family-owned-and-operated electrical contracting company servicing both residential and commercial projects, including wiring and lighting for new construction, additions, and repairs, since 2008.

Problem

The company was seeking to grow their business by doubling their revenue year over year but was having issues putting the right team and strategy in place to do so. Business had been stagnant with revenue hovering around $250,000 for the previous three years. The revenue profile showed only one major commercial client, and the remainder of the clients were primarily residential. How could Just It's Electric get more business and grow to a seven-figure entity?

Actions

In deploying the RFE, we looked at the financial history of the business over the last three years broken down into months. This provided a trend to see when business was at its best and worst. I instructed them to review the contracts and actions that contributed to their best months and develop a revenue plan strategy that matched their best month with the goal of duplicating that each month to meet the revenue-doubling format. We noticed that the easiest thing was to first stabilize the business. Since $30,000 seemed achievable and average, our first goal was to ensure we had steady business with at least $30,000 per month in revenue. This simple strategy would elevate the revenue of the business from $250,000 annually to $360,000 annually. This was not double, but it was consistent growth. In analyzing typical firms that provide electrical service, it is common for companies to grow by 1 percent per year, so employing this strategy effectively beat that 1 percent; however, that was not the entire goal. We needed more business and decided that there were opportunities in the government space and more opportunities in the commercial space. To get there, we needed more resources—salespeople, to be direct. We needed a salesperson for government focus, residential focus, and commercial focus with targets to bring the business into seven figures, and we needed to develop an overall plan with a target of $1 million to attack the market.

The focus then turned to the individuals in the business operations. The goal was to ensure the CEO worked on business, not in the business. First, we had to develop a plan to communicate the vision to the rest of the employees in the company. The CEO of this company had a frustrated vision as his team members were not on board with what he was trying to achieve. We had to fix that by determining the skill and will of each person in the organization to see if they fit the direction in which we were taking the company. We focused on hiring the right talent, especially an office manager to keep the rest of the organization focused. To help communicate the vision and develop the muscles for constant communication to the team, Jenkins & Associates provided a communication framework for weekly business communications. The first month of meetings were led by Curtis Jenkins so that everyone got used to the cadence. Business development was focused on getting more commercial and government business to meet the goal of doubling the revenue, so the owner partnered with more general contracting firms for more commercial business and got the necessary paperwork done to execute government projects. To maintain this momentum and prevent backsliding, Curtis Jenkins was hired as the chair of their advisory board to continue the process of running the business successfully over the next two years.

Outcomes

By using the RFE—first understanding the vision and communicating this vision regularly—the team was on board. Recognition of employees was always a strong suit of this company, and with added training, the employees were all in. The company is growing and is continually challenged to hire the right people. Jenkins & Associates continues to be a partner in helping to secure the right people to grow this business.

Testimonial:

"Jenkins & Associates provided Just It's Electric with the tools to realize the desired future of doubling revenues by getting the right people in place and working to execute the plan."

~ Erik Truxon, CEO, Just It's Electric

IT3

IT3 TECHNOLOGY CONSORTIUM

Introduction

T3 Technology Consortium is an information technology firm with a strong belief that corporate and community goals can be integrated in a way mutually beneficial for clients and benefactors who share similar values.

Problem

IT3 needed a disaster recovery strategy for its client, Howard University. The new CIO at Howard University discovered that their backup disaster recovery site was built on top of a restaurant. A restaurant fire could destroy all their data—the lifeblood of any company. IT3 won a bid with Howard University to provide a disaster recovery strategy but was uncertain about their approach and best-cost solution. They won the bid because they were the low-cost solution; however, once the bid was won, they needed help with the overall strategy and execution plan to deliver on the bid.

Actions

Jenkins & Associates was hired to provide help with developing an overall plan that supported the CIO's vision. The goal was to implement the solution in three months; however, there was a larger strategy required for a full solution supporting the new CIO. This first job was the test. During the first week, we met daily to develop the overall set of targets to meet the goal, focusing on vision, people, and a plan. This engagement was not focused on the cash flow as it didn't require much in terms of operations—yet.

Outcome:

After developing a sold plan and getting approval from the CIO, the plan was flawlessly executed. The seamless implementation of the backup system resulted in annual cost savings for Howard University and additional business for IT3.

This was one of the early experiences that began the foundation of the RFE. One of the primary values of the company was to provide 15 percent of the business's proceeds to charity. As a result, Curtis Jenkins became a partner in this business.

Testimonial:

"Jenkins & Associates helped IT3 'clear the fog' with the RFE and its heavy focus on the visualization and a clear, executable roadmap that delighted the customer resulting in additional business opportunities."

~ Rich Vivirito, Founding Member and CFO, IT3

ABOUT THE AUTHOR

Visionnaire Curtis L. Jenkins is a well-known author, entrepreneur, and project management executive. Having honed his expertise in project management for more than twenty years, Jenkins came to realize that everything in life is implemented twice: first as an idea or vision and second as a reality should someone have the audacity to execute on the vision. Project management is the basis of realizing every idea from concept to reality. An inspirational leader, Jenkins realized that the most important piece was getting everyone involved to visualize the same outcome. This would lead to motivated team members who are enthusiastic about the realization of the outcome. He quickly implemented this knowledge, fine-tuning his own projects to ensure the outcomes contribute to his vision. He soon realized there was no one-size-fits-all methodology but that bringing the vision to reality required creativity and soft skills. From that realization sprang the Realization Framework Experience™ and the vision for his latest book, *Vision to Reality*. Coming on the heels of his bestselling book, *The Only Job Search Book You Will Ever Need*, this new book helps those seeking career independence avoid the pitfalls of entrepreneurship and make their vison a reality.

Curtis L. Jenkins is a graduate of Temple University's Fox School of Business and Management where he earned his bachelor's degree in Business Administration. He later went on to earn his master's degree in management of technology from The Wharton School of the University of Pennsylvania in 2001.

Jenkins has served in many project management organizations where he mastered his proficiency in best practices technology and business enhancements toward cost optimization, revenue growth, and talent/leadership development. An expert in the development and utilization of process improvement principles, he has guided a number of businesses to achieve and surpass their company goals. In his most recent role, he managed business portfolios and IT projects, utilizing global talent and developing program management offices and projects for new companies.

As the founder and CEO of Curtis L. Jenkins & Associates, Inc. and Jenkins & Associates, Holdings, Curtis focused on real estate business ventures. Jenkins works with entrepreneurs to organize and drive themselves and their teams to focus on creating value. He is the acknowledged business ambassador in creating trust-based relationships and the organizational adoption of change strategies. In addition, Jenkins holds a Lean Six Sigma Green Belt (ICGB) and is a certified Project Management Professional. He is also a former President of BDPA Philadelphia, a nonprofit organization where he developed the talent to grow nonprofit businesses by focusing on the membership (people) and money (cash flow and fundraising). Curtis also served at the national level as

Vice President of Strategy and Planning and Membership Management where he used his RFE methodology to grow the organization during his tenure appointments.

A free ebook edition is available with the purchase of this book.

To claim your free ebook edition:

1. Visit MorganJamesBOGO.com
2. Sign your name CLEARLY in the space
3. Complete the form and submit a photo of the entire copyright page
4. You or your friend can download the ebook to your preferred device

Morgan James
BOGO™

A **FREE** ebook edition is available for you or a friend with the purchase of this print book.

CLEARLY SIGN YOUR NAME ABOVE

Instructions to claim your free ebook edition:
1. Visit MorganJamesBOGO.com
2. Sign your name CLEARLY in the space above
3. Complete the form and submit a photo of this entire page
4. You or your friend can download the ebook to your preferred device

Print & Digital Together Forever.

Snap a photo

Free ebook

Read anywhere

CPSIA information can be obtained
at www.ICGtesting.com
Printed in the USA
JSHW081429200223
37968JS00001B/28